RUSSIAN APPLIED ART

ART

Eighteenth
to Early Twentieth
Century

The White Hall of the
Mikhailovsky Palace (today
the Russian Museum) is
the only interior in Leningrad
dating from the first quarter
of the nineteenth century,
where the architecture and
the painted and sculptural
décor have been preserved in
their original state. Rossi
(1775—1849), who designed the
palace, was also responsible
for the interior decoration.

RUSSIAN

THE RUSSIAN MUSEUM, LENINGRAD

APPLIED ART

ART EIGHTEENTH TO EARLY TWENTIETH CENTURY

Aurora Art Publishers

Leningrad

Compiled and introduced by E. IVANOVA

Edited by V. PUSHKARIOV

Photographs by V. STUKALOV

Translated by Yu. NEMETSKY

Notes on the plates by

E. Ivanova (9, 26—34, 41—44, 47, 48, 89—91, 96, 109, 115—123, 126, 129—131, 139—147, 151, 152, 159, 163, 165, 167—169, 171)

I. Yasinskaya (2—5, 18—24, 35, 36, 39, 40, 49—58, 71—75, 86, 92—94, 97, 99—103, 105, 106, 110—113, 127, 128, 134—136, 149, 150, 157, 158, 160, 164, 170)

S. Rakhimova (1, 6—8, 10—17, 25, 37, 38, 45, 46, 59—70, 76—85, 87, 88, 95, 98, 104, 107, 108, 114, 124, 125, 132, 133, 137, 138, 148, 153—156, 161, 162, 166)

© Aurora Art Publishers, Leningrad, 1976

P $\dfrac{80104-561}{023\,(01)-76}$ 36-75

THE RUSSIAN MUSEUM was founded as a museum of fine art, but from its very inception in 1895 it acquired a number of superb items which had previously made part of the interior décor of the Mikhailovsky Palace — furniture, bronze candelabra, decorative vases carved out of coloured stone, and other *objets d'art.*

Immediately after the October Revolution the Museum began receiving works of art from the Winter Palace, nationalized private collections and other museums. These included porcelain, glassware, metalwork, bone and wood carvings, and also furniture and fabrics. By the end of the 1930s the Russian Museum's collection of applied art had attained the size and variety which characterize it today. The collection has in recent years been enriched by new unique specimens which constitute a source of national pride. New departments have been organized which were either non-existent before or, at most, were made up of a very limited number of exhibits. Today the Russian Museum in Leningrad is the only museum of Russian art to possess not only superb collections of painting, sculpture and drawing, but also an extensive collection of decorative and applied art. The artistic merits and the comprehensive character of many of its sections are beyond compare.

The present-day prestige of the decorative and applied arts section was not achieved overnight. At first a small part of the tapestries, mosaics, furniture, porcelain and bronzes was put on display in the Department of Painting. The first independent expositions of applied and decorative art were organized in the second half of the 'thirties. At the exhibition of 1957 objects of almost all the fields of Russian minor arts were represented. In 1960 the museum initiated a permanent exhibition of the decorative and applied arts of the eighteenth to early twentieth century, housing it in halls specially designated for the purpose in the right wing of the palace. Temporary expositions based on this or that part of the section's stocks are organized practically every year, adding to the viewers' acquaintance with the Russian Museum's collection.

The most prominent section of the Russian Museum's department of applied art is its collection of porcelain. Not only does it surpass all similar collections in other museums in the number of its pieces: it is marked by an unusual completeness and very high artistic merit as well. The better part of the collection consists of items created in the heyday of porcelain in Russia, covering the eighteenth and the first half of the nineteenth century. It was begun with the receipt of a large group of articles from the Hofmarschall's department of the Winter Palace, among them ceremonial table services of the time of Empress Elizabeth, items produced at the Imperial Porcelain Factory in St. Petersburg and at the privately owned Gardner Factory; many valuable pieces came from private collections, nationalized after the October Revolution.

In the last ten to fifteen years the museum's collection has been enriched with masterpieces produced by the Imperial Porcelain Factory in the first years of its existence. This period, which lasted from 1744, the year of its foundation, till the early 1760s, when production was reorganized, is closely linked with the name of Dmitry Ivanovich Vinogradov, an outstanding Russian scientist and an associate of Lomonosov. Articles produced within the period are known among Soviet art specialists as Vinogradov porcelain. There are around 250 items of Vinogradov porcelain in the Russian Museum, the largest collection of its kind anywhere. In 1746 Vinogradov, the father of Russian porcelain, created his first specimens, extremely modest little pieces devoid of decorative painting: cups, small bowls, salt-cellars and the like. Their distinguishing feature is the yellow-grey paste; here and there the glaze is blebby and the paste marred by black dots. Some of the samples are marked with the letter *W.* With the passage of time, having mastered the secret of porcelain, Russian craftsmen turned to more complicated tasks, shifting more and more of their attention to the artistic quality of their products. The tea-pots and jugs produced in the 1750s and early 1760s are a case in point. The decorative painting of Vinogradov's early works portrays mostly "exotic" subjects; in selecting his themes the master would often turn to China, the country where porcelain originated. This may be exemplified by the decorative sculpture series "The Chinese", also known as "People in Oriental Garb", as well as by two jugs, a dish and a vase.

By the 1760s the technical and technological difficulties of porcelain production had all been overcome. An outstanding creation of these years was the Imperial Factory's multiple table-set known in the history of Russian applied art as Her Majesty's Private Service (it belonged to the Empress Elizabeth). The majority of its items are housed in the Russian Museum: round dishes, lidded tureens, fruit baskets, soup, dinner and bread plates, mustard pots, knife and fork handles and porcelain spoons, which provide for a comprehensive picture of this magnificent ensemble's merits.

The shape of each item is round or oval; the baskets, vases and tureens are comparatively small in size and do not have any leg supports or platter-bases. There is a golden meshwork in relief with corollas of crimson flowers on each item.

The originality of the service lies in its independently conceived simple forms, the stability imparted to the items, the skilfully moulded décor and, finally, in the riot of colours typical of the Russian decorative arts.

Another of Her Majesty's private services, the gilded tea and coffee set, was produced at about the same time. In spite of the overall gilding the beauty of the articles, with their smoothly rounded lines, is perfectly evident. Some of the techniques used in the manufacture of Russian porcelain of the Vinogradov period were quite original. Thus, the openwork ornaments on vases and on the rims of plates were carved by hand before the porcelain was fired; applied details (flowers, figures on lids) were not moulded, as was the case with European porcelain, but actually hand-made. A singular technological device was the application of gold onto the porcelain surface. Finally, there was the remarkable device of first painting the design in red, then superimposing gold on the picture, which produced a décor slightly rilievo in quality.

The artistic merits of the Russian Museum's rich snuff-box collection far surpass those of similar collections housed in other museums. Each a miniature masterpiece, they are the very incarnation of elegance and beauty. The snuff-boxes on exhibit come in a variety of forms: shaped like an apple, like a cluster of grapes, a little chest or a shell. Popular at one time was the so-called packet or envelope snuff-box with a dedication or the owner's name written on its lid. Inside such boxes were gilded or adorned with the most graceful of decorative paintings. The best of these miniatures were done by Nikita Voinov and his brother Ivan. Often the snuff-box was set in a gold, silver or platinum mount and studded with tiny diamonds.

One of the most striking works in the museum's applied art collection is the Orlov service, produced in the Vinogradov period and so called because it was presented by Catherine II to Count Grigory Orlov. It consists of a tea set and a dinner set; everything matches: cups, saucers, tea-pot and the like go together with plates, knives and even toilet articles — a mirror and a scent bottle. The service was designed by A. Kozlov.

The oval medallions on each item carry the letters ГГО (Grigory Grigoryevich Orlov). The painted décor is made up of banners, drums and ribbons, the porcelain frame of the mirror is ornamented with tiny crossed cannons and little figures of Cupids.

There are traces of the baroque style in the form of the items, while the decorative painting is closer to classicism, with a preference for strict ovals, and a symmetry in the arrangement of the pattern.

The 1770s are marked not only by substantial improvements in the technology of porcelain production, but by the assertion of a new style in Russian porcelain, that of classicism. This is readily illustrated if we compare two scent-vases, one made in the 1760s, the other in the 1780s, designed to serve both as articles of interior décor and as vessels for aromatic substances.

The scent-vase of the 1760s is shaped asymmetrically: the body is decorated with ornamental scrolls, shells and flowers scattered over its surface at random. The 1780s vase, on the other hand, is distinguished by a strict silhouette; body, stem with base and neck with lid are precisely defined, the handles with a décor consisting of female heads are symmetrically placed.

Nowhere have the artistic ventures of the second half of the eighteenth century been more vividly exemplified than in the two enormous services known as the Arabesque service (1784) and the Yacht service (1780s), each of which comprised up to a thousand items. The Arabesque service also included, over and above this number, nine sculptures of a size suitable for table adornment. They would be placed in the centre of the table: grouped on both sides of a statue of Catherine II were the allegorical figures of Sovereignty, Philanthropy, Magnanimity, Justice, Military Might and Sea Power. The whole composition was conceived by the artist as a panegyric to the Empress and all she had done.

A participant in the creation of this grandiose ensemble was Jean-Dominique Rachette, who was responsible for the models for the decorative sculptures. It is also possible that he prepared the moulds for the individual pieces.

Following the canons of classicism, the Arabesque items are round, oval or triangular in cross-section. The ornamentation, which consists of arabesques and miniature medallions, details being picked out with gold, underlines the glittering white of the porcelain.

The Yacht set is an almost exact replica of the Arabesque as far as forms and colour scheme are concerned. The only distinctive feature in its décor is the emblem of the Russian merchant marine — the two-headed eagle and a white-and-blue flag.

It is not by the works of Rachette alone (and the museum has some productions by this master in biscuit) that one may judge of the porcelain sculpture of this period, but also by a sculptured series known as *The*

Peoples of Russia. This series owes its production to the book by I. Georghi entitled *A Description of All the Peoples Inhabiting the Russian State* (1776) and to a general interest in the life and mores of the people of multinational Russia. In contrast to the allegorical sculptures of Rachette, the figures of Estonian, Kirghiz, Yakut and other women are stocky, rather heavy and not meant to be viewed from all angles. Their clothes and ornaments are thickly painted on.

About the same time the factory produced miniature sculptures of hawkers, street-vendors and strolling musicians, similar in character.

By the end of the eighteenth century the Imperial Porcelain Factory's artists had evolved a new approach to porcelain as a material. Large-size items began to be produced, porcelain was combined with bronze and a layer of cobalt blue or green would be applied to the white porcelain ware. The smooth glittering surface of the porcelain, moreover, began to be regarded as a background best suited for the painted miniature. A case in point are the two unique sets for one, "solitaires", which belonged to Paul I and his wife. Also illustrative of eighteenth century porcelain are the works turned out by the first privately owned factory in Russia, which was established by Francis Gardner in the village of Verbilki in the Moscow province. Gardner's factory produced, among other things, tableware for popular taste with a painted décor of luscious purple flower-buds. As for the special wares created here, one of the most *recherchés* is the 1775 service with decorative painting by Kaestner. The curled forms of this ensemble's items and the manneristic décor show the influence of the rococo style.

The four services named for the Russian orders of St. George, St. Alexander Nevsky, St. Andrew the First-called (1770—1780s) and St. Vladimir (1785) were commissioned by the Imperial court. They were intended for use in the Winter Palace, when knights of the four highest Imperial orders were invited to dine on the feast day of the saint honoured by each order. The chief motif of the décor on these services was a reproduction of the order's ribbons, badges and stars intertwined with garlands of laurel leaves.

Compared to the sets produced by the Imperial Porcelain Factory, the Gardner ensembles are less elegant, though more picturesque: a reflection, no doubt, of the individual manner of Gardner's craftsmen. The most noteworthy items of the four "Order" services are the round and oval openwork biscuit-dishes with the painted décor representing, as in the former sets, the partic-ular order's badges, stars and garlands of ribbons. Apart from ribbons and orders, other leitmotifs appear in the decorative painting. An independent ornament was also introduced: wreaths of a soft green colour are to be found in the St. George set, and there is often an unopened flower bud or a little squirrel nibbling at a nut on the knob of the lid.

The early nineteenth century saw the establishment of a large number of privately owned factories, each distinguished by a style of its own. Their output consisted of items which, though familiar to everybody, were at the same time inimitable in their proportions, treatment of detail and colouring. Although crudely wrought, they were nonetheless charming in their décor and form.

In the nineteenth century the art of porcelain developed along the two lines discussed above: one as exemplified by the output of the Imperial Porcelain Factory, the other connected with the numerous private enterprises catering to the public at large.

The largest of the private enterprises was the Gardner Factory. In technical perfection, professional skill and artistic merit its output equalled that of the Imperial Porcelain Factory, which then had in its employ a number of outstanding artists and first-class craftsmen, many of whom had been trained at the Academy of Arts. One such artist in the early nineteenth century was S. Pimenov, who modelled a statuette of a girl with a yoke, dressed in a sarafan and wearing a *kokoshnik* on her head. This figurine (the famous *Watergirl*) subsequently became one of the most popular pieces to be turned out by both the Imperial Porcelain Factory and the Gardner Factory, as well as by minor potteries.

S. Pimenov was also the artist who designed the Guryev service (1809) which entered the Russian Museum in the 1920s. The colour scheme of this ensemble is based on offsetting the matted gold of the items' sculpted parts against the puce colour which covers almost the entire surface of each article. The function of the flawlessly modelled sculptural décor is to serve as a support for the vases, but so important is the role of the sculpture in every item that at times it seems they are not vases at all, but genre sculptures of Russian lads and lasses carrying a basket, dish or cup on their head or in their arms.

In the first quarter of the nineteenth century the Imperial Porcelain Factory was engaged primarily in the production of palatial table-sets and decorative vases. As a rule, they were covered with overall gilding and only the centre was left untouched to accommodate a decorative painting, such as a landscape, genre or mythological scene. During the 1830s the production of porcelain sculpture by the factory flourished, but by this time it was a sculpture which had lost its monumentality and strictness of form. This was manifested by the diminution of the figurines' size, their delicate modelling and the deliberate prettiness of the decorative painting. New works appeared portraying characters from popular plays and satires; statuettes of street vendors, servants and the like were also produced.

In the early nineteenth century the Gardner Factory put out a series of genre sculptures based on engravings published in the magazine *The Magic Lantern* (1817) and portraying popular Russian characters of the day, both city and country types. They now form one of the most significant and interesting parts of the Russian Museum's collection.

A. Popov's factory was renowned for its "tavern china" whose distinctive feature was a painted décor of bright flowers. There are almost no samples of this factory's mass-produced ware in the museum, but items individually conceived and made by Popov's masters are well represented. An especially interesting group is the factory's miniature sculpture: danseuses, the military, gentlemen in black dress-coats, maid-servants (some of the items are quite small, less than three centimetres high). One can spend hours viewing these exhibits, marvelling at the subtlety of characterization, the expressiveness of pose, the plastic beauty and the delicate modelling. The Popov Factory was famous also for the quality of its porcelain paste, so much so that Yusupov, the owner of a porcelain factory in the village of Arkhangelskoye (near Moscow), was a regular buyer of Popov's white porcelain. The vases, services, cups, etc. so received were then entrusted to Yusupov's artists, who decorated them with coats-of-arms, flowers, landscapes and views of Arkhangelskoye.

The produce of the St. Petersburg factory owned by the merchant Batenin is easily distinguishable from the porcelain of other factories in that its painted décor was always devoted to the theme of St. Petersburg. The factory's cups, gilded vases and services were ornamented with views of the capital's suburbs and architectural monuments. Batenin's artists also favoured a décor of red bouquets and green-leafed flowers painted in characteristic cold tones. The floral compositions were enclosed in a golden frame, which gave them a peculiar still-life look. Inimitable, too, are the gilded cups with their use of Chinese motifs in the décor.

Items produced by the Safronov Factory of the Moscow province were also very original. The services were often ornamented with faceting, gilding, blue and green coats of paint and a floral décor.

The factory's sculptors specialized in manufacturing amusing little figures of dandies and smartly-dressed women. These figures were realistic in appearance, and there was a touch of irony about them, as if the sculptor could not help laughing at the pomposity and smugness of these foppish young men or making fun of the overdressed ladies. Observing and recording the most typical and expressive traits, the craftsmen imparted a generalized aspect to the silhouette and devoted special attention to the decorative side from the point of view of colour.

The porcelain sculpture of the Kozlov Factory in the Moscow province was somewhat inferior to that produced by Batenin and Safronov, but no technical flaws can conceal the sincerity of feeling that went into the making of these figurines.

The second half of the nineteenth century saw the decline of porcelain production in Russia; by that time many privately owned factories had ceased to exist.

At the beginning of the twentieth century a number of outstanding masters of the pictorial arts tried their hand in porcelain. The work of Valentin Serov and Konstantin Somov in this field is represented by several sculptures. Porcelain turned out to be a highly appropriate material for Serov's sculptured group *The Rape of Europa*; the shine of the glaze serves to bring out more fully the peculiar plastic qualities of the composition. K. Somov did three subjects in porcelain: *Lady with a Mask*, *Lovers* and *On a Rock*.

The ceramics collection of the museum includes specimens of eighteenth century majolica produced at the Grebenshchikov Factory in Moscow, the St. Petersburg State Factory and the Gzhel Factory, though the number of these items is not too large. Majolica was the first material used by eighteenth century Russian potters to produce not only crockery but decorative sculpture and tiles. The Russian Museum's collection contains for the most part samples of crockery dating from the middle or second half of the eighteenth century. In them, the thick reddish-brown paste is concealed under a layer of bluish or yellowish-white opaque glaze. The painted décor of majolica consisted of flowers: in the case of the Grebenshchikov Factory the oval and round dishes and plates were decorated with blue bouquets placed in the centre. The Gzhel masters preferred birds and bright yellow flowers. In rendering the ornamentation, they would apply the brush in dabs and then outline the blotches in black.

The museum's collection also includes some Gzhel majolica toys: a wet-nurse, a musician with a balalaika, a cock, and figures of lions.

After the discovery in Russia of the formula for making porcelain and later, at the end of the eighteenth century, faience, interest in majolica as a material waned. It was only in the late nineteenth century that majolica was revived by the famous Russian artist M. Vrubel. Working in the ceramics shop of Abramtsevo, he created a series of majolicas on the fairy-tale themes of *The Snow Maiden* and *Sadko*, a portrait of an Egyptian woman, a vase and several decorative dishes. A new and effective decorative technique was evolved in this workshop: the item was glazed with a metal oxide which resumes its original colour after a special process of restorative firing, thus imparting an unusual metallic glitter to the ceramics. Such a decorative effect was especially suited to the unique plastic qualities of Vrubel's sculptures.

The Russian Museum's collection of faiences includes various items, such as crockery, vases, sculpted tiles, boxes, cache-pots, and decorative dishes.

Compared to porcelain, faience is a more modest material. It has a yellowish tint and is thicker than porcelain. Simplicity of form is a characteristic of faience, although in the nineteenth century the products of the best faience factories were in no way inferior to porcelain. The Russian Museum's collection includes a considerable number of items produced by the Kiev-Mezhigorye Factory, the largest factory of its kind in nineteenth century Russia. The red-and-brown and the light-blue services are shaped in the best traditions of classicism; the light-blue set is covered with a peculiar low-relief décor made up of corollas of miniature flowers. The white faience items made at the Auerbach Factory in the Tver province are noteworthy for the high quality of their paste, almost pure white in colour; they are ornamented with a painted blue décor of herbs and flowers. Equally interesting are the faience articles produced at the Poskochin and Golenishcheva-Kutuzova factories (St. Petersburg province), known as far back as the first half of the nineteenth century, when the ceramics industry attained a high stage of development. The Russian Museum's collection of artistic glass is as imposing as its ceramics collection and is considered one of the best in the country. It consists for the most part of goblets, decorative vases and services. Early eighteenth century Russian glass is represented by several goblets and cone-shaped tumblers embellished with monograms of Peter the Great. The tumblers are of a thick, opaque glass, ornamented and inscribed in an uncertain hand. The goblets, as a rule, have tall stems consisting, as it were, of faceted "apples". Beginning with the 1720s the engraved ornament was enlivened by gold, black and red paint. Not infrequently red and white filaments were fused into the stem of a goblet.

One of the collection's unique items is a tea-pot of transparent blue glass. Its spherical body is somewhat flattened, the handle curved into a light, sweeping loop, the spout, elegant in outline, is flawlessly positioned. The overall silhouette of the item fits into an imaginary oval, and the plastic qualities of the material are stressed by the tea-pot's elegant form. The rich blue colour does not diminish the transparency of the glass; on the contrary, combined with the gilding of the engraved ornament, it enhances the item's decorative aspect. Eighteenth century glass tea-pots are extremely rare and highly valued. The Russian Museum possesses several such pieces, but no two of them are in any way alike either in their proportions or in their details.

Beginning with the 1730s and 1740s glass began to be widely used as a decorative material in illuminatory appliances. A case in point is the candelabrum, a table-top illuminant with a ponderous décor of oak leaves made of cut glass. Later, in the second half of the eighteenth century, this abundance of massive cut-glass ornamentation gave way to stricter compositions of cut-glass pendants.

A popular device in mid-eighteenth century illuminants was the use of stained glass, red, cobalt blue or green, to fashion the baluster through which the main metal rod was intromitted.

The heyday of glass in the second half of the eighteenth century is inseparably linked with the name of M. Lomonosov. Experimenting in his workshop at Ust-Ruditsa (near Oranienbaum), Lomonosov and his followers busied themselves with the self-appointed task of revivifying the art of mosaics, so brilliantly developed in Ancient Russia and so undeservedly forgotten. Lomonosov was authorized by the Academy of Sciences to teach the art of stained-glass manufacture to the craftsmen of the Imperial Glass Works in St. Petersburg. His workshop was soon producing stained glass for mosaics, bugles and beads. Most of Lomonosov's surviving mosaics are housed in the Russian Museum; they include a portrait of Empress Elizabeth (from a canvas by Tokke), portraits of Peter III and Paul I, and several works by Vasilyev, a pupil of Lomonosov.

The scientist's experiments in glass gave an impetus to the emergence of a new and extremely interesting field of decorative art — embroidery in beads and bugles. This section of the collection consists of two groups identifiable not only chronologically, but by the character and function of their items. The museum houses two early buglework panels, both belonging to the second half of the eighteenth century. One of them, an elaborate composition, tells the story of Prometheus. Depicted on the second is a landlord's estate with peasants working on the land. The colour scheme is based on local tones of green, brown and grey.

Beadwork was unusually widespread at the time, and only items of artistic merit were selected for the museum's display. Outstanding among its handbags, wallets, purses, chibouk slip-covers and glass-supports is a wallet with portraits arranged in a chequered pattern. At the beginning of the century beadwork embroiderers favoured the lighter tones, white and pale-yellow, for the ground. Later, by the middle of the century, these gave way to darker tones; the compositions, mostly depicting fantastic plants, were overloaded with detail. By the end of the eighteenth century glassware items altered their form. That of the wine-glass, for instance, became more rigid. The ornamentation also underwent a change: miniature stars, rings or festoons of flowers were drawn in gold on red, blue or cobalt blue glass. The green and red wine-glasses with the monogram of Paul I may serve as an example; so can the tureens with cone-shaped lids. A most valuable item is the cache-pot of lilac glass with an inscription indicating its place of manufacture — the Nikolo-Bakhmetyev Factory in the Penza province. If one bears in mind that information relating to the glass works in Russia is very scant indeed, this item's value becomes all the more evident. Also referable to the late eighteenth century is a large blue decorative vase. It is a fine example of the free-blown glass technique. A glass-blower working in this technique could not have any definite pre-conceived shape in mind, so that the ultimate configuration of his creation depended solely on his skill and craftsmanship.

The history of Russian glass-making would not be complete without a mention of milk glass, reminiscent of porcelain for its colour and opaqueness. It was obtained by mixing bone dust with the ordinary vitreous mass. Items of milk glass share a resemblance with porcelain items in form and painted décor. The overwhelming majority of milk-glass articles in the museum's collection consist of tumblers, mugs, decanters, flagons, *kvasniks* (*kvass* bowls) and miniature vases.

Other interesting exhibits are several milk-glass decanters. These are deservedly rated among the best samples for their comely proportions and masterfully executed décor of purple flowers and garlands.

The impact of early nineteenth century classicism on glassware was not confined to new forms only. Decorative vases assumed such dimensions that it became necessary for them to be blown in several parts, which were afterwards fitted together. Items of transparent glass were covered with facets of a diamond cut, which gave them a heavier look. In large vases the cut glass was combined with an ormolu décor. For instance, the decorative egg-shaped vase of smoky lilac glass is covered with an intricate overall diamond pattern. The ormolu of the handles and of the rectangular base is harmonious with the soft lilac glitter of the glass. The Russian Museum's collection contains a number of large-size, elaborately designed glass table decorations, tabernacles and vases.

The growth of national consciousness brought about by Russia's victory in the War of 1812 was reflected in the artistic glassware of the time. Souvenir wine-glasses, tankards and decanters of colourless glass were often ornamented with portraits of war heroes, in the uniforms of their regiments, painted on white applied medallions. Particularly attractive is the cylinder-shaped wine-glass with a portrait of Kutuzov.

The Russian Museum's collection provides an insight into the changing approach to coloured glass in the nineteenth century. In the 1830s multi-layered glass became widely used. Craftsmen developed the technique of removing certain parts of one coloured layer after another and of constructing, in this way, elaborate patterns which not infrequently formed too heavy a décor.

Quite recently the museum's glassware collection was augmented by items of the multiple cut-glass service from "Alexandria", the Tsar's country residence in Peterhof. The cut glass of the service is colourless, faceted in a diamond cut and enlivened by little blue shields bearing the emblem of the residence. A closer look will reveal that certain changes in form have taken place and that there is now an overabundance of ornamentation: both facts must be regarded as a departure from the high classical style.

By the end of the nineteenth century glass as material had ceased to be the dominant element; the artist's skills were, so to speak, ousted by the perfected processing techniques. Vessels were made which imitated ceramics, wood and metal, and though this called for virtuoso skill on the part of the master it was all to the detriment of the item's artistic merit. Compared to this item, the elegant decorative vases ornamented with a décor of intertwined sprays and leaves seem more natural and more in harmony with the material. In appearance they share an affinity with French glassware produced at the glass works of Emile Gallé in Nancy: on the French articles the ornament was etched with hydrofluoric acid. The Russian masters executed their "Gallé" pattern by the more labour-consuming method of grinding the multi-layered glass.

The Russian Museum's collection of furniture is comparatively small. For the most part it consists of samples from palace interiors.

In the 1920s the museum acquired a large number of items from the Oranienbaum and Sheremetev palaces, from the Synod building and various St. Petersburg mansions.

Few art collections can boast of furniture pieces produced by Russian craftsmen in the early eighteenth century. The museum's leather-upholstered armchair is a magnificent example of furniture of the Petrine epoch. The beauty of the piece lies not in its ornamentation but in the plasticity of its forms, in the smooth transition of one line into another, and in the way the craftsman utilizes the artistic possibilities of finely polished oak.

The rational atmosphere of the first quarter of the eighteenth century, which was reflected in interior decoration, gave way to a marked preference for luxury in the second half of the century. By the end of the 1740s an elegantly playful rococo style had asserted itself. The most interesting items in the museum's collection of furniture pertaining to this period are a carved and gilded side-table and two mirrors in gilded wooden frames. The console seems to be woven of scrolls and spiral shells and fanciful flowers smoothly flowing into each other.

Like all other furniture, mid-eighteenth century mirror frames were covered with gilding and ornamented with an elaborate rocaille décor.

Housed in the Russian Museum is part of a large suite of furniture designed by Rinaldi, the illustrious eighteenth century architect, for the Chinese Palace in Oranienbaum (now the town of Lomonosov in the Leningrad Region). This furniture is outstanding for its highly expressive silhouette and beautifully wrought details. In spite of some very obvious elements of the rococo (the smoothly curving lines of the backrests and frames of the chairs, the characteristic rocaille scrolls), this Rinaldi suite is distinctly classical in style. The carved

ornamentation is relatively modest and is arranged symmetrically, most of the details devoid of carved décor. Among the more remarkable pieces is a bureau bookcase from the Chinese Palace. The lower part of the bureau consists of drawers with *bombé* walls, while the top serves as a clock-case, with carved and gilded volutes on both sides (this type of décor brings to mind an architectural structure). The bureau is painted bright blue, and this intensely coloured surface serves as a background for the *fêtes galantes* depicting ladies and cavaliers in eighteenth-century dress.

In 1965 the Russian Museum acquired a roll-top desk of the utmost rarity. It is made of mahogany and decorated with marquetry in ivory and wood of various species. Engraved on an ivory plate inside one of the drawers is an inscription giving the maker as J. G. Kohl, a Petersburg master otherwise completely unknown. This mahogany desk illustrates the transition period which Russian cabinet-making was undergoing in the 1770s. The tranquil and severe neo-classicism which superseded the rococo style had not yet been finally established, and in this piece we find echoes of the rococo: the curving legs, the serpentine contours of the top and the *bombé* sides of the drawers. At the same time the form of the cylinder lid, the flat top with a bronze balustrade, the brass strips setting off each part of the desk are all commensurate with the principles of neo-classicism. The traditional elements and the new classical forms are here integrated.

There is a great variety of furniture in the museum's collection appertaining to classicism in its heyday, and amply illustrating it. The collection includes light and elegant Jacobean furniture decorated with copper inlay, gilded suites comprising a large number of items, bean-shaped work-tables embellished with inlaid ornaments, console-tables, secretaires of different shapes and sizes, and many other articles. The Russian cabinet-makers of that time invented all kinds of new forms of furniture adapted to this or that requirement of living: they could in this way give rein to their imagination.

The four carved late eighteenth century side-tables in the museum's collection all have stretchers lavishly decorated with sculptured compositions, which proves once again that the Russian cabinet-makers of the time had a predilection for embossed carving.

In the late eighteenth and early nineteenth centuries the public's interest shifted to furniture of more stocky proportions (this is evident above all in the armchairs and settees of the period); gilded embossed carving was introduced. Examples of this are furnished by a mahogany suite dating from the first half of the nineteenth century. The elbow-rests of the armchairs and the settee of this suite are carved in the shape of swans and painted to imitate old bronze. The metallic rosette onlays, the rectangular and rhomboid insets, the "shoes" which support the legs, the embroidered pictures inscribed in a circle on the upholstery are all reminiscent of the furniture produced by Voronikhin.

Gilded carving was not the only form of ornamentation in Russian furniture of the second half of the eighteenth century. The less ceremonial, everyday furniture was, as a rule, polished and inlaid with wood of various species. The museum houses but a small number of items of this type: several bean-shaped tables with inlaid table-tops and the so-called "Tver desk", dating back to 1770. The top, sides and drawers of the desk are decorated with views of the town of Tver (now Kalinin) painted from engravings. The outward forms of the piece are simple enough, while inside it there are many drawers and secret compartments. The inner surface of one of the secret doors is ornamented with a painted basket of bright flowers. One gets the impression that all this wealth of drawers and pigeon-holes was conceived by the master chiefly to accommodate the skilfully executed decorative paintings which determine the artistic value of the Tver desk.

The Russian Museum's collection of furniture consists for the most part of items dating from the first quarter of the nineteenth century: these are the Empire suites from the Mikhailovsky, Winter and Yelagin palaces. The collection is attractive in the wide variety of its forms, décor and materials. In addition to gilded furniture there are many pieces of furniture in Karelian birch, poplar and mahogany.

The works which laid the beginnings of the museum's applied art collection are all linked with the name of Rossi. Outstanding among these is the carved and gilded suite of furniture which graces the museum's most handsome interior — the White Hall. We can see here a brilliant example of the realization of Rossi's artistic principles, when all elements of the décor, including furniture, are subordinated to the general architectural concept. The gilded carved ornamentation adorning tables, armchairs and sofas—all those wreaths, stylized acanthus leaves, rosettes and palmettos—harmonizes with the painted walls and ceiling, which are decorated with the same motifs. The architect's concept was implemented by the painters Ange and Scotti, the parquet craftsmen Bobkov and Zimensky and the cabinet-makers the brothers Bobkov.

The so-called Haute-lisse suite of the Winter Palace (early nineteenth century) seems to embody the ideals of high classicism. The majority of the items in this suite are now in the possession of the Russian Museum. Of particular value is the original upholstery, the so-called "chair" tapestries, which were produced on special order at the St. Petersburg tapestry manufactory.

A highly original instance of the art of furniture-making in the early nineteenth century is a mahogany settee whose décor displays the traditional Empire motif of helmet, sword and shield, treated in a novel manner. It is not a large settee, with the soft bolsters giving it a certain intimacy.

The Russian Museum's furniture collection consists not only of sets from palatial interiors: there are a number of sets from Russian country mansions as well. The forms of this furniture were also influenced by the classical style. The most frequent materials employed were mahogany and Karelian birch, and there are fewer instances of ornamental gilding.

In the first quarter of the nineteenth century Russian craftsmen created an elegant and comfortable type of armchair with a trough-shaped backrest which adapted easily to the curves of the human body.

In the second half of the 1820s high classicism reached a point of crisis and was superseded by an eclectic period in which all the previous styles mixed freely together. "Second rococo" and pseudo-Gothic influenced the making of furniture in this period, and there were also other styles, such as "à la russe". The museum has in its possession only a few such pieces, most of them being the work of well-known masters, as the architect A. Stakenschneider and the painter V. Vasnetsov, or coming from the famous Tour furniture shop. Furniture produced at the joiner's shop on the estate of Abramtsevo near Moscow is represented by original items whose forms and décor are borrowed from old peasant art.

The museum's collection of Russian fabrics is rather small, although highly valuable, including as it does a considerable number of tapestries. The tapestries were the first items of the Applied Arts Department to be displayed at the Russian Museum before October 1917. The beginnings of the collection were laid in 1908 and 1910, when the museum received some tapestries from the collections of the Grand Duke Sergei Alexandrovich and the Ekaterinhof Palace, among them portraits of Peter the Great and Catherine II, the tapestries *Bathsheba*, *The Eagle*, *Time Freeing Faith of Its Fetters* and *Still Life* by Vavoque.

The Imperial Tapestry Factory, founded in 1719, was in existence till the mid-nineteenth century. Its productions were designed to adorn the ceremonial chambers of palaces. The first Russian tapestry produced at the factory by one of its first weavers, Vavoque, was not very large and was in all probability copied from a Dutch still life.

Tapestries were either woven after cartoons specially executed for the purpose, with decorative compositions or mythological scenes, or they reproduced the works of well-known painters from the Hermitage collection.

The large tapestry *The Battle of Poltava* (1724) executed by Bégagolle after a cartoon by Caravacque is a characteristic example of the art of the time, which glorified heroic exploits and reflected important historical events.

Many of the tapestries in the museum bear woven inscriptions with the name of the master and the date of execution. The inscription on the tapestry *Bathsheba*, for example, reads: "Made in St. Petersburg by Russian apprentice in 1727". A 1733 tapestry is signed by Master Anton. The excellence of the tapestries in the museum's possession stems not only from the evident professional skill of the weavers, but also from the artistic merit of their productions.

The tapestry *Bathsheba* is characterized by generalized forms and local colours; the scene is portrayed, as it were, in close-up. In *The Eagle* an attempt is made to imitate a painter's tenuous brushstroke, with the resulting silverish-grey half-tints. The abundance of detail makes the tapestry resemble a painted canvas. Another interesting example is the large, vertically elongated tapestry *Africa* (1749) belonging to a carpet series called *The Parts of the World*.

Mention should also be made of the "chair" tapestries which were used to adorn and upholster furniture. Some of them carry depictions of baskets with flowers, woven into others is a stylized ornament.

The tapestries of the second half of the eighteenth and early nineteenth century include many portraits: Count Shuvalov, Potemkin, the Empress Elizabeth. The last named tapestry is outstanding for the beauty and delicacy of its colour scheme.

The technology involved in the production of a tapestry was an extremely complex one: suffice it to say that the craftsman saw the right side of the carpet only as it was reflected in a mirror, otherwise in order to check the accuracy of the pattern and the colours he would have had to walk around the frame of the loom. A square metre of tapestry took from one and a half to two years to complete. Large-size tapestries were usually worked on by several masters.

By the late eighteenth century Russian weavers had attained such a degree of skill that even today their creations cannot but arouse admiration for their technical perfection, colour and elaborate composition.

In the first half of the nineteenth century Russian weavers favoured themes reflecting important historical events. The *Liberation of Greece*, a tapestry of incredible beauty, may serve as an example.

The small-size carpet of unassuming colours, *Telemachus* (late eighteenth century), was, to judge from the technique employed in its making, produced in a privately owned workshop, not at the Imperial Factory. Telemachus is depicted talking to Calypso. The contours of the figures are accentuated by a dark line, and this produces an impression of flatness. The landscape is subordinated to the plane of the carpet. In spite of the abundant ornamentation, the colours of the tapestry are distinguished by delicate nuances. The combination of blue, brown and muted yellow tones creates a gamut seldom seen in eighteenth century Russian tapestries.

Another tapestry in the collection, a narrow piece designed for the pier between two windows and depicting a tree in a tub, is stylistically close to *Telemachus*.

Very popular in the first half of the nineteenth century were woollen shawls with a floral ornament on both sides, skilfully woven by women. They came into fashion at the very beginning of the century and were called Kolokoltsov shawls after the name of one of the workshop's proprietors. It was, however, generally believed that the very best shawls were manufactured by the workshop which belonged to the merchant woman Merlina where skilful female serfs worked as weavers.

The Kolokoltsov shawls were woven of the finest wool from a specially bred strain of sheep. Only a few Kolokoltsov shawls have survived: the Russian Museum has about twenty in its collection.

Shawls of an earlier period were either soft blue or white, with a border of varicoloured flowers. One is positively amazed at the delicate nuances of colour in the ornament of the blue shawl with a Merlina workshop mark; the impression is that this is the work of a water-colourist, not a weaver.

In the late 1820s and early 1830s the colour of the shawl changed, the favourite now being red; the woven border was usually composed of cucumbers interspersed with flowers.

The woollen scarves were sometimes stitched into one piece from strips of various colours, red, yellow and white, which impaired the former wholeness of these items. By the mid-nineteenth century the art of making the Kolokoltsov shawl gradually died away.

Silk kerchiefs with a brocade ornament constitute another part of the museum's collection of fabrics. The ornament, which covered the entire surface of the kerchief, was woven in gold or silver thread on a red, green, violet or sometimes black background. These brocade kerchiefs share an affinity with the embroidered sarafan in the character of their ornament and the technique of their execution.

Most of the kerchiefs in the museum were made at the factory near Moscow belonging to the Levins, and this is proved by the ciphered trade mark woven along the edge. These kerchiefs are graced by a golden, seemingly "chased" ornament; their decorative merit is equal to that of other outstanding creations of Russian applied art of the eighteenth and the first half of the nineteenth century.

The Russian Museum's collection of artistic metals, like its fabrics, does not aspire to a fullness of representation and cannot compete in this respect with larger collections in other museums. The exhibits of this section consist of objects wrought in precious and non-ferrous metals — gold, silver, copper, bronze and brass; these are mostly illuminants and tableware, tobacco boxes and furniture pieces. The earliest items are of gilt silver and date to the mid-eighteenth century. The most outstanding specimen of the group is a tea and coffee service with distinctly baroque forms. The tea-pots and coffee-pots have complicated, irregular shapes. The chased scrolls and shells impart a whimsical air to the items and the high quality of the slightly lustrous gilding enhances the expressive and plastic effect of the ornamental relief.

The museum's collection was recently augmented with a presentation *kovsh* (scoop) of the mid-eighteenth century. Its boat-shaped form is traditional; the décor is composed of a chased applied ornament.

The most numerous group in the metalwork collection consists of tureens with lids. Round and oval, these convex lids are adorned with figures of Cupids, fruit or flower buds which often constitute the only ornamentation on an otherwise smooth surface.

The art of the gunsmiths of Tula is represented in the collection by caskets, mirror frames and candlesticks. There are also some furniture items made by Tula craftsmen — a table and an armchair.

In 1965 the museum acquired a collection of 40 samovars. After this the Applied Arts Department devoted much effort to building up its non-ferrous metals collection, and it now has considerably more samovars.

Unlike porcelain, glass, bone and silver items, old copper samovars never attracted collectors. Notwithstanding, quite a number of these articles have come down to our day. At first they were acquired mainly by local history museums; today even museums of art are showing an interest in the samovar.

The history of the Russian samovar leads us back to the eighteenth century. Its original form was that of a tea-kettle with a chimney. A copper samovar of this type can be seen in the museum's collection; it has a coat of brown patina and the hallmark of a Nizhni-Novgorod coppersmith. In the course of its two-hundred-year-old history the samovar was fashioned in a host of beautiful and diversified forms. Some of them (e.g. the Tula samovar of the Chernikov Brothers' factory) preserve the classical forms of eighteenth century vases, others, such as the kind favoured by travellers, were shaped like a cube with detachable legs.

As time passed the form of the samovar changed, and with it such details as the tap, handles and supports, which were fashioned in the shape of dolphins, curved stalks, twigs, fruit, etc. Russian coppersmiths knew how to give their metal an unexpected hue. That is why side by side with red copper samovars we see in the collection golden-yellow brass samovars and samovars with a coat of greenish or sometimes brownish patina. The collection also includes a small group of bronze clocks. The rarest, almost the only one of its kind, is a large early nineteenth century clock with a figure of Peter the Great. It is elaborately ornamented, its sides embellished by low reliefs reproducing important events in the life of Russia in the eighteenth century.

New acquisitions have been made in recent years to expand the non-ferrous metals section. These include, among others, a clock produced at the Olonets factory (mid-eighteenth century) in the shape of a Gothic cathedral with two standing figures. Every detail of the clock is modelled with the most delicate accuracy; the general shape of the composition is highly expressive, even though it is fashioned out of the "difficult" material of cast iron.

A brief survey cannot hope to tell the whole story of the Russian Museum's minor arts collection. It may, however, add to the reader's knowledge of the artistic culture of the Russian people and of those nameless virtuosos whose creations, so numerous and so diverse, are housed in one of the largest repositories of art treasures in the country.

PLATES

First half of the 18th century

←
1. Tumbler and goblet. First quarter of the 18th century

Very few glassware articles dating from the first quarter of the eighteenth century
have come down to our days: that makes the extant goblets, wine-glasses, bottles
and tumblers all the more valuable. The traditional form of the goblet remained practically
unchanged throughout the eighteenth century: all goblets had a cone-shaped body
decorated with an engraved pattern, and a long baluster-like stem. The vegetal
ornamentation usually surrounded the medallion. Sometimes a short text was introduced
instead of (or in addition to) the ornamental composition. The conical shape of the
tumbler was also very popular in Russian glassware of the first quarter of the eighteenth
century. The ornamentation of the piece reproduced consists of military attributes.

2, 3. Tapestry: "The Battle of Poltava". 1723
This battle-piece tapestry is one of the first
creations devoted to a historic subject to be
put out by the Imperial Tapestry Factory.
In the foreground, represented against a panorama
of the battle, is the figure of Peter the Great in
the uniform of an officer of the Preobrazhensky
regiment.

4. Tapestry: "Fruit on a Table". 1717—20
This tapestry is one of the earliest
creations of the Russian tapestry industry.
The drawings used to decorate tapestries
were extremely diverse, often with works of
painting serving as originals.
In the still life reproduced here one
seems to recognize some work by a master
of the Dutch school. Woven along
the edge of the tapestry is a blue border.
The author of this work, the master
J. Vavoque, came from France together
with other craftsmen of the State Gobelin
Factory, invited to work in Russia.

5. **Tapestry: "Bathsheba at the Fountain".** 1727
This tapestry was executed after a cartoon by an
unknown master. The subject is taken from Rubens'
Bathsheba at the Fountain, painted around 1635.
The tapestry is an interesting specimen not only
for its consummate craftsmanship but also
because it is one of the first works of its kind
executed by a Russian master.

6. Gospel cover. First quarter of the 18th century

Book covers of precious metals were often embellished with stones or insets of coloured glass. Compositionally and in its interpretation of the images this cover is reminiscent of Russian wood-carving of the preceding centuries. The high quality of the chasing is most evident in the ornamentation on the back of the cover, where large succulent fruits in rectangular medallions alternate with typical eighteenth century garlands of leaves.

7. Bowl. First half of the 18th century

The earliest known silver vessels of cylindrical shape resting on low supports of the claw-and-ball type belong to the beginning of the eighteenth century. The motifs of the engraved décor and the combination of niello and gilding are here still very much like those current in Russian applied art of the eighteenth century.

8

9

8. Tumbler with lid. 1738
The tall conical drinking vessel with
a lid was quite common in eighteenth
century Russia. Engraved on the
one reproduced is a traditional
ornament: a medallion with a genre
scene. The rest of the surface area
is taken up by sumptuous baroque
scrolls and pinnate leaves.
The knob of the lid is in the form
of a fruit with leaves.
This ornamentation was typical of
mid-eighteenth century silverware,
porcelain and faience.

9. Tea-pot. Late 1730s
The tea-pot depicted creates a striking impression by its
perfectly proportioned forms and elegant silhouette.
The craftsman, displaying his natural sensitivity
to the feel of material and desirous of bringing out
the beauty of the glass, combines a succulent blue
background with the engraved and gilded-over ornament
(the monogram under the Russian Imperial crown
and the tulips). For the late 1730s this piece is highly
remarkable, since the manufacture of coloured
glass really flourished only in the second half of the
eighteenth century when the workshop of Mikhail
Lomonosov, the great Russian scientist, began putting
out coloured glass for mosaics, bugles and beads.

10. Goblet. 1740s

In the mid-eighteenth century
the traditional form of the goblet
underwent a change: the contour of
the stem grew more intricate.
Moreover, the engraved ornament on
the surface of the glass was either
gilt or enamelled in black.
This was especially conducive to
revealing the finish of the glass and
enhancing its lustre. By blowing air
bubbles into the glass material an
additional play of the faceted surfaces
was attained. The body was usually
ornamented with coats-of-arms and
monograms. The areas in between were
given over to a vegetal decoration
consisting of flowering shoots
alternating with military attributes.

11. Goblet. 1730s

In the mid-eighteenth century a new
method of ornamenting glass came
to be known in Russia. The technique
was to coat the glass with a red
lacquer, cover it with gold foil,
draw the design, and then cover it
with another layer of thin glass.
Along with the gold spot in the
central part of the composition
the goblet is embellished with the
traditional engraved ornament, which
was arranged around the medallion.

12. Goblet. Mid-18th century
This goblet with narrow
vertical facets attracts
attention by its unusual
ornamentation, which
consists of parallel bands
of cut oval notches on both the
body and stem of the vessel.
The refraction of the design
pattern in the facets of the
transparent glass produces a
charming effect.
The engraved medallions
are compositionally executed
in the eighteenth century
tradition of glass decoration.

13. Bottle. Mid-18th century
The bottle is adorned with
baroque scrolls and a delicate
trellis ornament.
The two round medallions
on the bottle's sides enclose
a monogram and a portrait
of the Empress Elizabeth
Petrovna of Russia.
The pretentious letters of the
monogram and the
curving lines of the bizarre
leafed branches are vividly
illustrative of the rocaille
type of ornamentation.

14

14. Book of Psalms cover. Second quarter of the 18th century

The cover is chased all over with fine ornament — grapes and ears of corn amidst
rocaille scrolls; garlands of leaves and flowers are executed in high relief. The maker,
Nikolai Don, a St. Petersburg silversmith, was known as the creator of a number of
works of high artistic merit.

15. Tureen from Peter the Great's dinner service. Mid-18th century

The production of silver services began in Russia in the first half of the eighteenth century.
They consisted of many articles, among which were tureens of various shapes.
By the middle of the eighteenth century the larger articles of ceremonial dinner services
had acquired new shapes with complex patterns, in which chasing and casting played
a major role. The sumptuous vegetal ornament with figures of animals and birds imparts
a festive appearance to the tureen reproduced here.

16. Tea-kettle. 1764

The second half of the eighteenth century was for
Russian art a period marked by the rise of classicism.
This silver tea-kettle, however, is visible proof
of the fact that Moscow masters were still producing
works typical of the declining rococo style: the kettle's
surface is covered with scrolls, shells and cartouches.

17. Goblet. 1750s
The production of silver
goblets in Russia reached its
peak in the eighteenth century.
Goblets were made in a great
variety of shapes and were
highly valued as presentation
pieces. Foreign goldsmiths and
silversmiths who came to work
in Russia in the course of
the eighteenth century
opened workshops and gave
their apprentices a thorough
training. The hallmarks found
on the articles show
that they often worked
together, producing highly
original objects decorated with
Russian motifs.

18. Tapestry: "Wild Animals Fighting at a Watering-place". 1747

This tapestry is a variant of François Deporte's once well-known composition
The Fight of the Animals. The ornamental motifs of the Russian tapestry are, however,
more laconic and generalized than those conceived by the French artist.
Compared to the tapestries created at the beginning of the eighteenth century, the piece
is larger in size and is intended for the sumptuous décor of an interior in the baroque
style. The border of the tapestry imitates a carved gilt frame.

19

←

19. Side-table and candelabrum. Mid-18th century
Side-tables, compositionally united with the wall,
first made their appearance in Russian palatial interiors
in the second third of the eighteenth century.
The table reproduced is adorned with asymmetrically
arranged carved and gilded volutes, stylized acanthus
leaves and flowers. The intricate forms of the legs
and table-top and the rocaille motifs in the painting
on the black background of the table-top are all
characteristic of Russian minor arts in the mid-
eighteenth century. The candelabrum on the side-table
is described under No. 25.

20. Mirror. Mid-18th century
In mid-eighteenth century palace interiors a major role
was assigned to mirrors in gilded carved frames.
Their asymmetrically arranged volutes, shells and
rosettes harmonized with the decoration of the furniture.

21. "Chair" tapestry. 1750s
Besides tapestries with reproductions of genre pictures,
still lifes and portraits, others intended to serve
as upholstery for furniture were also produced.
These were called "chair" tapestries. The well-balanced
composition and symmetrical arrangement combined with
the ornate scrolls of the cartouche permit this item
to be regarded as a production of the transition period.

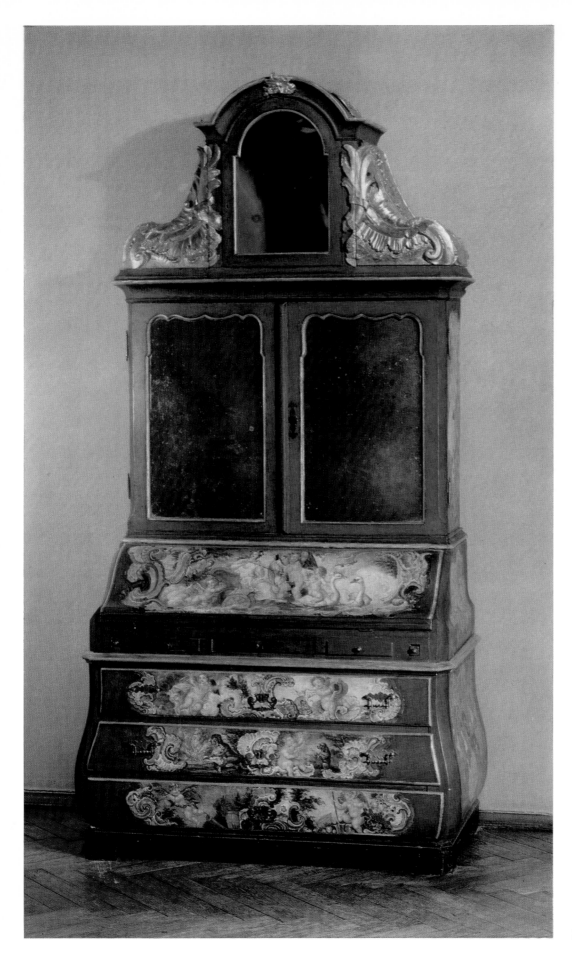

22, 23. Bureau bookcase. 1740—1750s
The upper part of this bureau bookcase
served as a clock case. The combination of
polychrome painting with gilded carving
is typical of mid-eighteenth century
Russian furniture. Depicted on the front
side, in addition to mythological scenes,
are the personages of La Fontaine's fable
Le Singe et le Chat.
On the lateral sides of the bookcase are
panels portraying scenes of *galanterie*.

24. Mirror.
Second half of the 18th century
The mirror decorated with acanthus leaves and other elements pertaining to the style of classicism is surmounted by two volutes, a typical feature of the baroque.

25. Candelabrum. Mid-18th century
Mid-eighteenth century candelabra were often executed in the form of a fantastic tree with crystal adornments in the shape of large oak-leaves with faceted edges. The typical colour of Russian glass of the period was lilac. The light of the wax candles was reflected in an effective manner in the crystal pendants of the candelabrum. Similar candelabra can be seen now in the Museum of Ceramics and Glass at Kuskovo and in the Palace Museum at Ostankino, both near Moscow.

26. Snuff-box. Second half of the 18th century

Porcelain snuff-boxes were especially widespread in the eighteenth century. Among the most
popular were envelope-shaped snuff-boxes bearing the name and sometimes the address of the owner,
and even "sealed" in imitation of real envelopes.
On the inner side of this round snuff-box's lid is a portrait of Catherine II as Minerva.
In the 1750s snuff-boxes were often executed in the shape of an apple, a cluster of grapes or a shell and
decorated with painted panels showing allegorical and genre scenes, still lifes and landscapes.

27. Biscuit-dish. Early 1760s
The wicker-basket form of the dish is traditional.
In this case the openwork pattern is reminiscent of
a garden fence. The analogy with architectural forms
does not, however, undermine the intimate character
of the article.
Russian masters executed the openwork
design on vases and plate rims by hand, incising
the pattern on the piece before firing.

28. Special bowl for wine-glasses. 1750s

Bowls for wine-glasses, filled with
warm or cold water (depending on
how warm or cold the beverage should be),
were used to serve the guests.
In the mid-eighteenth century they
were oval-shaped, with fluted sides, and
were ornamented with painting
representing flowers, landscapes, birds
and animals. Not infrequently the
motif of the painted décor would be
an allegorical scene.

29. Scent vase. Late 1750s

Scent vases filled with fragrant substances
whose aroma spread all over the room through
the slits in their lids were usually placed on
side-tables and made part of the interior décor.
The form and ornamentation of the vase reproduced is characteristic of the rococo style.
This is due above all to its asymmetrical shape
made up, as it were, of fanciful
shells and scrolls. The material properties of
porcelain, its plastic beauty and the lustre of
its surface, are here ingeniously utilized.

30, 31. Items from Her Majesty's Private Service. Late 1750s

This dinner service commissioned by the Empress Elizabeth Petrovna (hence its name) is considered to be the first multiple table-set produced at the Imperial Porcelain Factory. All its items are abundantly ornamented with a moulded pattern. An important role in the décor is assigned to the gilded relief network with corollas of red flowers and the hand-moulded garlands. The service's distinctive aspect stems from the simple forms of its items and the inimitable richness of the ornamentation which is so typical of Russian applied art. In the history of Russian porcelain-making this service is regarded as a superb sample of its early, so-called Vinogradov period.

32, 33. Items from the Orlov service. Early 1760s

The service was ordered by Catherine II for Count Grigory Orlov, her favourite, in connection
with his appointment to the post of chief of artillery of the Russian army. The author
of the ornamental design, Kozlov, introduced trophies into the décor, such as banners,
crossed cannons and bombs, placing beside them figures of Cupids and rocaille scrolls.
The service contains not only such items as a tea-pot, tea-caddy, plates, knives, forks,
spoons, etc., but also a toilet mirror and caskets. Most of the set's items, including
the porcelain-framed mirror, are kept in the Russian Museum, but a few can be found
in the Hermitage and in the Museum of Ceramics and Glass at Kuskovo near Moscow.
Some more articles are housed in a private collection at Hillwood, Washington. The Orlov
service is one of the most outstanding creations of the Imperial Porcelain Factory;
it completes the Vinogradov period in the history of Russian porcelain-making.

Second half of the 18th century

34. Perfume vase. 1780

This vase is one of a series of four perfume vases found
in the Russian Museum, Leningrad. The four vases,
evidently executed for some palace interior, are identical
in form and ornamentation; only the miniatures in the
medallions are different. A considerable part of the
decorative painting is done in gold.
Vases of this type, pertaining as they do to the style
of classicism, are reminiscent of amphorae. An important
role in their decoration was assigned to the floral
garlands and the medallions suspended on ribbons.
The miniatures in the medallions usually
depicted allegorical scenes.

→
35. Desk. 1779

The fronts of the drawers and the surface of the roll
top are decorated with the panels portraying pastoral
scenes, skilfully inlaid with ivory and wood of various
species. On the inside of a pigeon-hole door is the
representation of a woman with sword and shield,
the latter bearing the master's signature and the date.

→
36. Tapestry: "Venus Riding Dolphins". 1763

In its intensity of colours and the variety of ornamental
forms this tapestry is a typical mid-eighteenth century
creation, although it must be said that the motifs
of antique mythology and the romantic treatment of
the landscape could pertain to works of an earlier period.
Venus Riding Dolphins is one of the few signed tapestries
indicating the date, manner and place of its execution
and the name of the craftsman responsible.

37, 38. Candelabra.
Late 18th century

The manufacture of cut-glass candelabra attained its peak in the second half of the eighteenth century.

They were produced in a great variety of forms: in the shape of a vase topped by little cut-glass pyramidal figures; with garlands so arranged as to form an openwork crystal hemisphere, etc. Each little crystal was intricately faceted and was secured by thin wires.

This made for an arresting play of the sparkling lights.

39. Panel: "Picnic". Second half of the 18th century

Along with mythological subjects, beadwork embroidery
of the second half of the eighteenth century often
depicted scenes of *galanterie* as well. The ladies
in vivid garb under the canopy and the peasant
binding sheaves of a radiant yellow form an expressive
group whose decorative character is enhanced by the
pale opaline background.

40. Panel: "Prometheus". Second half of the 18th century
Depicted on the panel is one of the myths about Prometheus.
The light background, the black contours of the composition's
prime elements and the decorative aspect of the colouring
which distinguish this piece are all typical of beadwork
created in the second half of the eighteenth century.
The buglework embroidery of the panel is done without cross-
stitch canvas and reminds one of satin-stitch embroidery.

41. Dish. Second half of the 18th century

In the second half of the eighteenth century the small town of Gzhel became a prominent centre
for the manufacture of majolica. Potters employed at workshops and small factories used the local sorts
of clay, renowned for their special qualities, and produced articles marked by a plastic expressiveness of
form. Their painting technique was based on a combination of dabs of bright colour, yellow, green, blue
and violet, with black graphic lines. The motif of the drawing on the dish is the one frequently used by Gzhel
craftsmen to decorate their wares — a cock amid trees and flowers.

42

42. Tea-caddy. Second half of the 18th century
White was the colour most often used in enamelled
articles since it helped to achieve a resemblance
of the latter to expensive porcelain ware.

43, 44. Tiles. Second half of the 18th century

Tiles were widely used in the eighteenth century for facing stoves and wall panels;
the interiors of Peter the Great's Summer Palace in the Summer Gardens, Leningrad, may
serve as an example. In the second half of the century tiles were produced in Moscow,
St. Petersburg, Kaluga, Tula, Vologda, Veliky Ustiug, Yaroslavl and other Russian cities.
However, we have no exact information as to the place where the tiles reproduced here
were manufactured. Usually tiles were painted over in enamels of three to five colours;
the themes were predominantly genre scenes, landscapes, flowers. Not infrequently motifs
for the decorative painting were taken from the book *Symbola et Emblemata*, and from
calendars and primers. Sometimes the pictures would be accompanied by an explanatory text.
By the end of the century painted tiles were supplanted by white faience plates in relief.

45. Tray. Second half of the 18th century
Enamel-coated copper plates and dishes were
intended to replace porcelain ware,
which in the mid-eighteenth century was very
expensive. The dazzling white enamel
surface was overlaid with an openwork
ornament of silver. It was customary to
include turreted walls and artillery pieces
into the traditional vegetal pattern.

46. Coffee-pot and tea-pot. 1780
Enamels, predominantly of blue or
green tones, were widely used in
the manufacture of copper tableware.
Particularly interesting in these
items is their applied stamped silver
ornamentation.
Articles made to order were often
adorned with monograms enframed
by scrolls in the baroque style.

47. Tureen. Second half of the 18th century

The most popular motif in eighteenth century porcelain tureens were bouquets
of flowers, beetles and butterflies. Ornamentation of this kind was also widely used
in Meissen porcelain. However, the Russian painter's manner is felt in the soft outlines
and delicate nuances of colour. Porcelain tureens were as a rule round or oval; their
lids were sometimes capped by a flower bud or a lemon cut in half.

48. Kvass jar. Second half of the 18th century

Among the numerous similar items produced by the Imperial Porcelain
Factory this one is remarkable for its resilient contours, the plastic expressiveness
of its relief-ornamented details and the high degree of craftsmanship
evident in its painted décor.

49, 52, 53. Items from the Arabesque service. 1784

The Arabesque ceremonial dinner service consists of 973 articles. One of the most original creations of Russian applied art, it is marked by a strictness and plasticity of form and a symmetrically arranged ornamentation based on elements of antique decoration — the so-called arabesques.

51

←

50, 51. Table ornaments from the Arabesque service. 1784

The Arabesque dinner service included nine sculptural groups commemorating in allegorical form Russia's victories on the battle-fields and in the sphere of diplomacy. These decorative pieces were made after models by Rachette, specially approved by the Academy of Fine Arts. *Justice* (No. 50) is shown as a woman in antique dress with a book in one hand and fasces, symbol of authority, in the other. The gilded scales symbolize the equity of the law. The composition *Sea Power* (No. 51) portrays Amphitrite, a sea goddess, with a dolphin; the full armour of a warrior standing in the bows of a ship completes the allegory.

53

54—56. Items from the Yacht service. 1780—1790s

The Yacht service was modelled after the Arabesque service, repeating its forms and the arrangement and colour-range of its ornamentation. Almost all the items of the service are decorated with highly original designs on blue medallions: eagles clutching laurel wreaths and flags with crossed anchors (the emblem of the Russian Merchant Navy). Like the Arabesque, the Yacht service is one of the factory's outstanding achievements in the second half of the nineteenth century.

**57, 58. Porcelain statuettes: "Estonian Peasant Woman" and "Kazan Tartar";
"Bagpiper Boy" and "Peasant Girl Selling Berries".** Second half of the 18th century

The statuettes reproduced are part of a series which renders in porcelain the engravings of I. Georghi from the book *A Description of All the Peoples Inhabiting the Russian State* (1776). Some art historians — N. Wolf (1906) and Y. Danko (1938) — attribute the series to Jean-Dominique Rachette, others — B. Emme (1950) and A. Saltykov (1962) — think that Rachette only supervised the work.

59, 60. Jug. Sugar-basin.
Second half of the 18th century

Milk glass first appeared in the second half of the eighteenth century to imitate porcelain, the production of which at that time was a costly undertaking. Objects of milk glass were akin in form to the glassware items of the period. There is a tranquillity and fluency in their outlines, their surfaces are rounded, the knobs of the lids are usually fashioned in the shape of fruits with leaves. The ornament is reminiscent of the decorative painting on porcelain: bouquet of flowers with a dark red rose in the centre.

→
61. Goblet. Mid-18th century

The large-size engraved ornament of the goblet is combined with the faceted cutting in its lower part. Etched within the medallion is a monogram; the inscription indicates that the goblet belonged to Alexander Golovkin, one of Peter the Great's associates. By the mid-eighteenth century Golovkin had already for some time been in disfavour, and it would seem quite unlikely that this presentation goblet was produced at the Imperial Glass Works. Besides, the engraving technique and the quality of the glass are such as to indicate that it was made at a private factory.

62. Goblet. Second half
of the 18th century

The shape of cut-glass
goblets remained
unchanged throughout
the eighteenth century,
whereas the ornamenta-
tion became increasingly
intricate: frequently the
engraved pattern would
cover almost the whole
surface of a goblet. The
faceted, somewhat heavy-
looking base of the goblet
reproduced is counter-
balanced by the solid
decorative frieze around
the rim.

63. Kvasnik (*kvass* bowl). Late 18th century
The *kvasnik* is a cylindrical vessel for
kvass which resembles a large mug. *Kvasniks*
were very popular at the end of the eighteenth
century; in form they followed the rules of
classicism, the décor consisting of palmettos and
circular bands of pearl-like ornament. The applied
medallions of milk glass were also decorated
with painting.

64. Bowl. Late 18th century
Articles of coloured glass with decorative
painting in gold, silver and enamel were held in
great esteem in the second half of the eighteenth
century. Floral garlands, bands of geometrical
figures, miniature stars scattered in checkerboard
order — these patterns in the ornamentation
are typical of classicism. The articles are designed
in modest, streamlined forms with smooth curves.

65. Part of a set for wine and fruit.
Late 18th century

The Orlov set for wine and fruit was produced in the late eighteenth century. The articles of the set clearly reflect the classical trend of the end of the century and present mainly rounded forms with a vertical facet in their lower parts. The thin transparent glass is painted over with garlands, bands of geometric figures and leafed floral branches placed here and there.

66. Wine-glasses. Late 18th century

The manufacture of coloured-glass items achieved its heyday in the late eighteenth century. However, articles of red and green glass were comparatively rare. The golden décor of garlands, leaves and scrolls, which was widely current in the last quarter of the eighteenth century, served to underline the depth and intensity of the glass's colour. Many articles were made to order and adorned with the owner's monogram.

67. Toilet mirror.
   18th century
Toilet mirrors were often
mounted in intricately shaped
frames of carved ivory.
One is struck by the superb
craftsmanship that went into
the carving of the shells, the
festoons of beads, and the
openwork ornamental panels.
The panels with mythological
scenes were affixed onto a
lining of multicoloured foil.

68. Cup. Second half
   of the 18th century
Working on ivory, the carvers
preserved the traditional form
of the goblet — a cone-shaped
body and a tall stem — and
ornamented their articles with
openwork or relief carving.
Arranged around the
medallions were climbers and
rocaille shells. Subjects were
usually borrowed from the book
Symbola et Emblemata and
were rather freely interpreted
by the carvers.

69. Panel with portraits. Second half of the 18th century

Some of the ivory carvers of Kholmogory (province of Archangel) were talented masters of the portrait. The refinement of modelling, the clear-cut contours of the jugated profiles and the overall laconicism of the composition were achieved by using red foil for the background. Typical of these works was a frame made up of rectangular plates of contrasting colours, embellished with floral designs, and rocaille ornamentation.

70. Casket. Second half of the 18th century

Plates of ivory, usually painted, were glued to the wooden base of the casket. They were arranged symmetrically, so as to form frames around carved insets with hunting scenes, animals and birds. The combination of different-size coloured plates and carved ornamentation added to the casket's decorative qualities.

71, 72. Bean-shaped table and detail of its décor.
   Second half of the 18th century

The table is inlaid with light and dark-coloured woods.
In the centre of the bean-shaped table-top is a panel.
These small portable tables were used for reading and
needlework.

73—75. Desk and details of its décor. 1770s

The desk is one of the few known early works of its kind. The surface of the collapsible top, inlaid with wood of various colours but of one species, is decorated with a geometrical ornament. The panel in the centre of the top represents a panoramic view of Tver (now Kalinin). Other views of the town are on the three sides of the desk.

74, 75

76, 77. Mirror, candlestick and casket. Inkstand.
Late 18th century

In the second half of the eighteenth century the
craftsmanship of the gunsmiths of Tula, creators
of unique art pieces in steel, attained the peak
of perfection. The polished surfaces of their
items were embellished with cut reliefs and with
incrusted garlands of flowers in gold.

78. Potir. 1794
The production of silverware became especially widespread in the second half of the eighteenth century.
It is manifested above all by the development of the art of niello which allowed to embellish the articles with complex compositions on religious or secular subjects, depending on the item's function. The space between the thematic compositions was usually taken up by vegetal ornaments.
The nielloed images stood out clearly against the gilded ground, which was frequently covered with engraved patterns.

79. Gospel cover. 1775
The repoussé cartouches in the four corners of the cover contain symbolic images of the four evangelists. Represented in the centre is a scene from the gospel. The sumptuous décor of the cartouches, the treatment of the figures of the evangelists and the trellis background are characteristic of the baroque style.

80. Snuff-box. Late 18th century

In the late eighteenth century the Veliky Ustiug masters turned to new motifs in the ornamentation of their pieces. The map of Vologda province on the lid of the snuff-box bespeaks the affection felt by the master and his contemporaries for their native places. The map was executed by F. Bushkovsky, one of the best silversmiths, carvers and nielloists of the town of Veliky Ustiug. Only the inside of the snuff-box is gilded, which is typical of silverware produced in that period.

81. Tea-pot. Second half of the 18th century

The role of purely ornamental motifs in silver articles produced in the second half of the eighteenth century was comparatively small, since the décor was generally based on thematic compositions copied from engravings and drawings. The silver tableware, with its *bombé* sides, was no exception. The tea-pot reproduced is ornamented with wavy lines engraved on a gilded background, a design specially favoured by Moscow masters.

82. Flask. 1774

Tobolsk, one of the largest towns in Siberia, was in the second half of the eighteenth century a prominent centre of the production of silverware. Many articles were executed by Tobolsk masters for the Governor of Siberia, Count Dmitry Chicherin. Particularly interesting are the items dating from the 1770s when the silversmiths, retaining the old forms, decorated their articles with a niello ornament. The rocaille scrolls form a kind of frames enclosing emblems, monograms and elements of vegetal decoration. The rich ornament, produced by niello on a gilded ground, alternates with plain silver strips. The lid, handles and other details of the articles were often adorned by cast silver twigs with flowers and fruits. The lower and upper parts of the flask reproduced are decorated with a meander pattern.

83. Tankard and cup. Mid-18th century

The Russian copper-processing industry in the Urals attained its peak in the middle of the eighteenth century. The Demidov works, for instance, produced various brass utensils: pitchers, mugs and cups. The surface of many items was ornamented with high-relief chasing.

84. Samovar. Late 18th century

The samovar first appeared in Russia in the eighteenth century, when tea-drinking came into fashion. Executed in the form of a vase with intricately shaped handles, samovars were often adorned with chased bands of vegetal décor consisting of floral garlands and bouquets. The tap in the form of a dolphin illustrates one of the most favoured decorative motifs of the time.

84

85. Kvasnik. Second half of the 18th century
The cylindrical form of the *kvasnik* reproduced is accentuated by the horizontal
garlands of flowers and the gilded bands with dark red roses. The decorative painting
was usually arranged round a centre-piece landscape, portrait or monogram.

86. Part of the service with views of the Pavlovsk park. Late 1790s
The service consisted of six items of cobalt blue porcelain elegantly ornamented with
patterns in gold and miniature paintings. The themes of the paintings are variations of
water-colours by Sylvester Shchedrin or engravings of his works. Similar miniatures
adorn the porcelain top of a table at present in the Pavlovsk Palace.

87. Tea-pot. Second half of the 18th century

The first privately owned porcelain factory in Russia
was founded by Francis Gardner in the village of
Verbilki, Dmitrov district, Moscow province.
Porcelain articles produced for sale by the Gardner
Factory were simple in form, the only embellishment
being polychrome painting. A typical Gardner
pattern consists of miniature lilac and blue flowers
with large red roses in the centre or baskets of
flowers. Gardner's items are always easy to recognize
due to their bright colours, the comparative
simplicity of the composition, the flat representation
and conventional character of the painted motifs.

88. Part of a tea set. 1775

By the late 1770s the Gardner Factory came to be widely known. The themes of the decorative painting of the set reproduced are connected with the recent victory of Russian arms, the signing of the Kuchuk-Kainardji peace treaty on July 30, 1774. They present in allegorical form Russia's military might and sea power. The set was painted by J. Kaestner who worked at the factory from the day of its foundation. These vividly coloured miniatures, which witness to Kaestner's consummate craftsmanship, are framed by a scroll ornament with bouquets of flowers.

89. Part of the St. Andrew dinner service. 1777—80

In 1777—85 the Gardner Factory turned out ceremonial dinner sets named for the four highest Russian orders of St. George, St. Andrew the First-called, St. Alexander Nevsky and St. Vladimir. The décor of these services comprised elements of the order concerned—the badges, stars and ribbons arranged on a white background. The dish's rim is adorned with a relief in the shape of the order's chain. The delicately moulded openwork, the highly decorative character of this set's items allow them to be ranked among the factory's most significant artistic pieces.

90. Part of the St. Alexander Nevsky dinner service. 1777—80

A special *élan* is imparted to the service by the painted red *moiré* ribbon, beautifully adapted to the various shapes of plates, salt-cellars, creamers, etc.

91. Part of the St. Alexander Nevsky dinner service. 1777—80

The dishes of the service are fashioned in the rather unusual form of a tree leaf. Their somewhat naturalistic painting is relieved by a red *moiré* ribbon.

92. **Coffee set.** Late 18th century

The "calico print" ornamentation of little golden twigs stresses the modesty and simplicity of the set's décor.
The lost items of the set were replaced by replicas created in the first quarter of the nineteenth century as indicated by the mark on the creamer.

**93. Bowl for wine-glasses from
the Cabinet service.** Late 1790s

The Cabinet service, an enormous
ceremonial dinner service created in
the late eighteenth century, consists of
800 articles. The marks indicate that
some of the articles were manufactured
in the early nineteenth century. While
the forms of the items are classically
strict, the decorative painting is done
in a sketch-like manner. The landscape
motifs and the patterns of wild
flowers are typical of the period.

94. Vase. Late 18th — first third of the 19th century

On the pale green background of the vase's body is a square painted medallion
with a view of the wooden theatre erected by architect S. Shustov in 1827 on Kamenny
Ostrov (Stone Island) in St. Petersburg. The other side of the vase is decorated with a
painted caduceus, an attribute of Hermes, framed by gilded stylized acanthus leaves.
The squat form of the vase, the applied band of small beads along the rim of the lid and
the stylized fruit on its top are all characteristic of late eighteenth century porcelain.

95. Vase. Early 19th century
This unusually shaped decorative vase presents a rather rare combination of coloured and milk glass. The shape of the transparent green sphere is typical of glassware in general; the foot and neck of the vase, similar in silhouette, are of milk glass. The ornamentation consists of miniature roses and gilded trefoils. In this it is similar to the décor on the porcelains then being produced and illustrates the vivid and colourful displays so favoured by Russian applied art and so typical of its items.

96. Egg-shaped vase.
   1796—1801
The body of the egg-shaped vase is affixed to a bronze tripod on a round marble base. The soft outlines of this piece, the expressive plasticity of its forms are illustrative of the artistic devices peculiar to the applied art of the second half of the eighteenth century. The bronze handles with volutes impart a graphic clarity to the vase's silhouette. The delicate, somewhat dry decorative painting is concentrated in the two medallions with architectural landscapes and four horizontal bands.

97. Toilet table. Late 18th century

Mahogany came into fashion in Russia towards
the end of the eighteenth century. The variety
of tones and the rich lamellar structure of mahogany
made it ideal for the manufacture of furniture.

98. Candelabrum. Late 18th century

The candelabrum reproduced illustrates a type much favoured in late eighteenth century Russia. It consisted of a globe-like or vase-shaped central part made of transparent glass and a brass hoop to which the candlesticks were affixed. Cut-glass flowers on bronze stems inserted into the "vase" imparted a particularly festive look to the piece.

99. Vase. Late 18th century

Besides the mahogany
veneering and the technique
of marquetry current at the
end of the eighteenth century,
art objects made of wood were
frequently decorated with
gilded carving. The vase reproduced evidently served as table
ornament. Its massive base
is decorated with palmettos
in low relief. The openwork
bowl of the vase, an example
of the most delicate craftsmanship, is supported by female
figures in antique dress.

**100. Tapestry: "Telemachus
Recounting His Exploit
to Calypso".** Detail. Second
half of the 18th century

The tapestry's theme is
borrowed from a once popular
novel by François Fénelon
*The Adventures of
Telemachus, Son of Ulysses.*
The colour scheme, the
treatment of the landscape,
the use of thick woollen
thread mingled with fine gold
thread, the bilateral weaving
all suggest that the tapestry
was done at a privately owned
manufactory.

ТЕЛЕ
МАК РОСКАЗ
ВАЕТ СВИЮ
ПОХОЖЬДЕ
ЯНЕ КАЛИ
ПЗ С Б

101

101, 102. Bracket. Clock. Late 18th century
The seven-candle bracket and the clock are carved out of wood in the traditions of
Russian classicism. The coat of gilding reminds one of tinted bronze, a technique
current in the Russian applied art of the time. Also characteristic of the style
of classicism, apart from this decorative device, are the swan (central part of the
bracket) and the Bacchanal scenes (bas-reliefs on the base of the clock).

⟶

103. Cloth. Fragment of a chasuble. Late 18th century
The prevalent ornamental motif on the cloth is a vegetal pattern with inwoven variegated
silk and brocade threads. The compositional arrangement of the ornamentation
is characteristic of the 1790s.

104. Vase. Early 19th century

Voronikhin (1760—1814) and masters of his circle are well known not only as architects, but also as designers of large-size decorative stone vases. Differently shaped bowls of these vases usually had supports in the form of tritons, snakes or human figures. Particularly popular in this respect was the dolphin. The combination of decorative sculpture and the shell-shaped bowl of the vase and the clever choice of material testify to the author's rich creative imagination.

105. Embroidery. Fragment of a chasuble. Late 18th century

106. **Cloth.** Fragment of a cope. Late 18th century

19th — early 20th centuries

107. Vase. First quarter of the 19th century
The entire surface of this monumental vase of
thick pale-lilac glass is deep-faceted. The diversified
faceting was widely used to bring out the specific
qualities of the flint glass — its glitter and
iridescence. The vase's handles in embossed ormolu
are decorated with mascarons.

108

108. Toilet table and mirror. First quarter of the 19th century

The toilet table was made for the dressing-room of the Mikhailovsky Palace. The décor consists
of female figures in antique dress supporting heavy festoons of flowers, two horns of plenty, sphinxes
and vases. The combination of the ormolu and the dark blue of the smalt table-top with the quiet,
muted tone of the mirror's silver frame points to the author's superb taste. The early nineteenth
century saw the flourishing of the artistic fashioning of bronze, and this enabled Russian architects
working in the field of minor arts to implement many of their ideas.

109. Vase. First quarter of the 19th century
Crater-shaped porcelain vases were
first produced in Russia in the 1820s.
In the course of the first half of the
nineteenth century their proportions and
the character of their décor underwent
quite a number of changes. The smooth
surface of these large items was taken
up by paintings copied from works
by Western European and Russian artists.
Usually a team of painters worked on
a vase: one was responsible for the
landscapes, another for the ornamentation,
a third for the gilding, etc. The painting
on the vase was often framed by a
geometric ornament. The remaining parts
were covered with green or blue paint,
and over these an engraved gilded décor
would be applied.

110. Settee. First quarter of the 19th century
This settee is ornamented with relief carving
gilded to resemble dark antique bronze.
The décor consists of trophies so favoured by
classicism. These, together with the colour
range, lent furniture an air of ceremonial
solemnity and monumentality.

111, 112

111. Chair. First quarter of the 19th century

This chair of simple forms with the gilded carving in low relief on a white background has an air of solemnity typical of Empire style furniture.

112. Chair. Early 19th century

The chair was part of a ceremonial suite specially made for the Winter Palace. Some of the items of the suite are now housed in the Hermitage, Leningrad, and the Tretyakov Gallery, Moscow. The legs of the chair are decorated with gilded carvings in relief; the back presents an example of openwork carving. The seat is upholstered with tapestry executed in the haute-lisse technique (the weaving of wool with silk).

→

113. Carpet. First quarter of the 19th century

This floor carpet is one of the rarest creations of early eighteenth century Russian carpet-making. The ornament in the form of a trellis entwined with rose twigs shares an affinity with the decorative painting of the time. It has been suggested that the carpet might have been done after a drawing by Rossi who rebuilt the Yelagin Palace in 1818—22 and was responsible for its interior décor.

→

114. Vase. 1819

Large ornamental gilded vases with handles in the shape of female figures are typical of Russian applied art dating to the first quarter of the nineteenth century. Such vases were usually decorated with paintings depicting rustic scenes.

The artists' interest in the life of the common people is a noteworthy phenomenon, though the images of the peasants in these paintings are somewhat idealized.

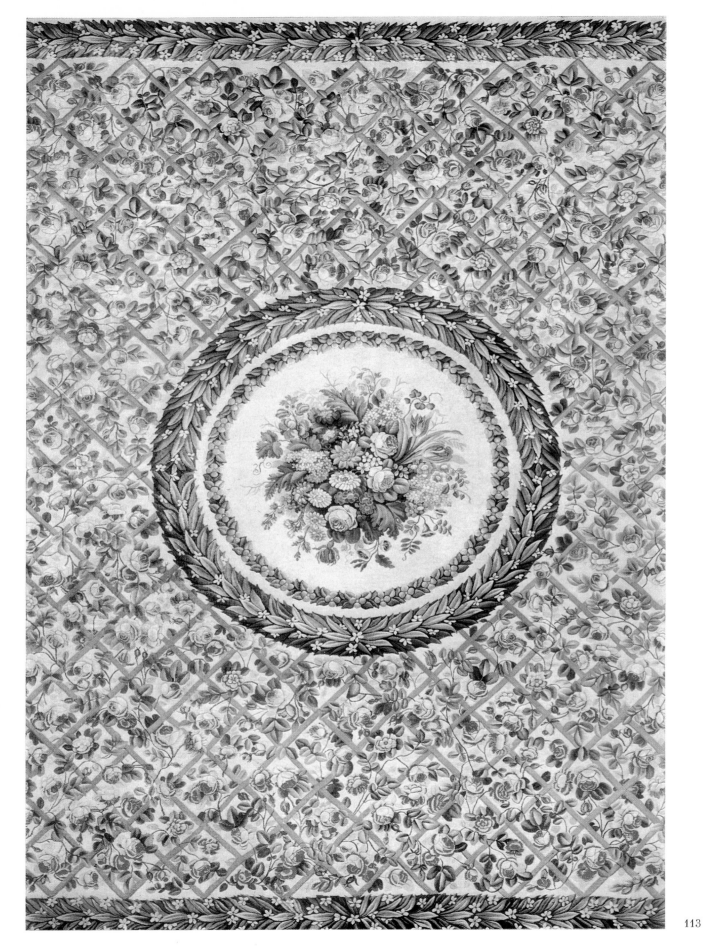

115

115—119. Items from the Guryev service. 1809

The service owes its name to Guryev, the manager of the Emperor's private chancery, who placed the order with the Imperial Porcelain Factory. In the opinion of B. Emme, the service was in use from 1848 on at formal dinners in the Peterhof palace.

The creation of the service is probably linked with the name of S. Pimenov, an outstanding Russian sculptor, professor at the Academy of Arts, who headed the sculpture department of the Imperial Porcelain Factory from 1809. The high artistic merit of the sculpture decorating the vases of the service seems to confirm this supposition. The miniatures which adorn the items were painted after engravings, oils and water-colours produced by late eighteenth and early nineteenth century artists. Throughout the nineteenth century new items were being constantly added to the service to replace those lost; as a rule, they bore the factory's mark. The later items differ from the earlier ones in the way the ornament is arranged along the plates' rims; the painted miniatures are less ornate. By the end of the nineteenth century the service numbered 4,500 items. The major part of them are today housed in the Pavlovsk Palace near Leningrad.

118

120. Part of the Green service. 1830s

This elegant tea-cum-coffee service for two consists of nine items and is distinguished by the exquisite silhouettes of all the pieces, by superbly modelled relief rims, and by the virtuoso decorative painting in gold on a rich green ground.

121

121. Cup and saucer. First quarter of the 19th century
The cup resembles a crater-shaped vase. Its lid is unfortunately lost. The two handles are decorated in the lower part with miniature floral relief. The painted medallion represents Terpsichore. The handles, base and body are fixed together with the help of special pins (the technique used in the making of large porcelain vases). The saucer rests on a high foot and the whole composition has a remarkably festive look.

122, 123. Tumbler and goblet. Goblet.
First quarter of the 19th century

After the victorious end of
the War of 1812 the Imperial Porcelain
Factory and the Bakhmetyev factory
produced a whole series of articles
(tumblers, mugs and wine-glasses) devoted
to the heroes and events of that war.
Worthy of mention are several pieces of
colourless cut glass with facets
of a diamond cut, and with horizontal
or vertical facets, all with applied
medallions of milk glass. Portrayed on the
items reproduced are the celebrated
military leaders of the 1812 War.

124

124. **Toilet set, paper-weight and table ornament.**
First half of the 19th century
Art objects in malachite combined with ormolu and cut glass display the high degree of craftsmanship achieved by Russian masters.

125. **Candelabrum.** First half of the 19th century
The candelabrum reproduced attracts special attention in that the acanthus leaves, lyres and laurel branches of the décor are made of bronze and combine effectively with the cut-glass garlands of oak leaves. The combination of two materials in one item, in this case glass and bronze, was quite popular in the early nineteenth century.

126. Clock case. 1849

This square-shaped clock case is supported on the shoulders of a kneeling Cupid.
The front of the pedestal carries a relief composition with naked figures of children
(which could imply the transience of time).
Faience was widely used in the nineteenth century for the fabrication of clock cases,
no less frequently, in fact, than wood or metal. The faiences put out by the Kiev-
Mezhigorye Factory between 1798 and 1850 were renowned for their high quality. The
relief ornamentation, in particular, is worthy of mention. A number of items — dishes,
plates and jugs — were covered all over with a low relief ornament of flowers and leaves.

127

127. Cloth. First half of the 19th century
The ornamentation of this decorative cloth
is characteristic of the style of classicism:
large, well-defined stylized bouquets
arranged in checkerboard fashion.

128. Kerchief. First half of the 19th century

The ornamental design of this kerchief consists of a symmetrically arranged vegetal pattern of thin, leafed, vine-like branches, flowers and clusters of berries. The effect produced by this item is due to a special variety of gold thread forming narrow glittering stripes. The letters inwoven along the border indicate the place of manufacture. In the late eighteenth century and throughout the first half of the nineteenth the Levins' factories in Kolomna and Moscow were in the front ranks of the country's silk-weaving industry.

129. Porcelain statuette: "Girl with a Pitcher". First quarter of the 19th century

This porcelain figurine is a typical example of small-size sculpture produced at the Imperial Porcelain Factory in the first quarter of the nineteenth century. Its comparatively small dimensions, the body's elongated proportions, the clothing, the matt surface of the porcelain and, above all, the evident desire to convey the beauty of the Russian peasant woman are all features which this item shares with the works of S. Pimenov — the sculpture pieces of the Guryev service (pl. 115), the *Peasant Lad* (pl. 130) and others.

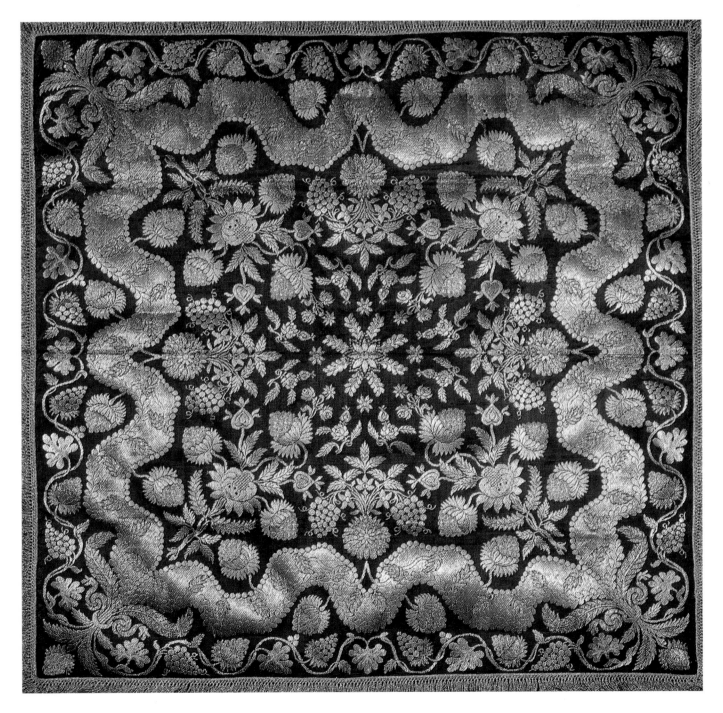

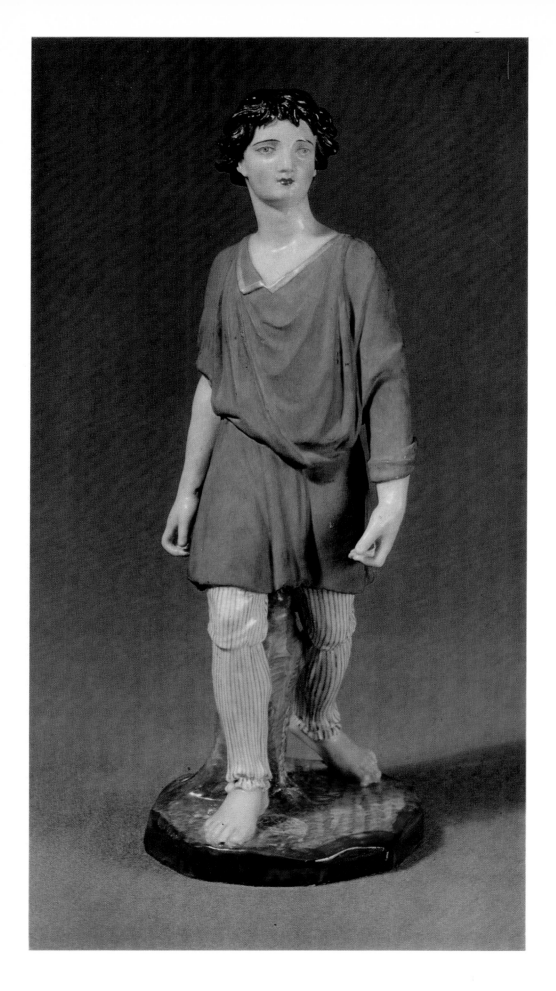

130. Porcelain statuette: "Peasant Lad". 1810s

In style the statuette shares an affinity with
the sculptures of the Guryev service (see pl. 115),
which allows it to be considered a work by S. Pimenov,
though definite evidence on this score is not available.
Compared to the gilded sculpture pieces of the Guryev
service the statuette looks more realistic. This is due
to the character of the painting aimed at
producing a "real life" effect. The statuette embodies
the physical and moral beauty of the Russian peasant.

131. Dish. 1810—1820s

The Novy brothers' small factory near Moscow
produced porcelain and faience wares. Their
décor was often borrowed from engravings which,
in the opinion of B. Emme, were so modified
in the process that it is sometimes difficult
to establish what original they were made from.
The scene reproduced on this dish is painted in
cobalt blue and apparently goes back to a book
illustration. It is surrounded by a floral wreath.

132. Tankard. 1835

In the first half of the nineteenth century
precious metals were used predominantly in the
manufacture of decorative and presentation items.
The development of different techniques enabled their
makers to turn to new methods of ornamentation.
One of these consisted in arranging stamped
figures of *putti* or of people in antique dress around
the mugs, tumblers and tea-pots, with the rim of
the object ending in a rolled band of bunches
of grapes and grape leaves. The handles and lids often
had knobs in the shape of antique heads, wreaths or
basketfuls of fruit. The strictness of form,
the lucidity and dignity of style, the surface not
overloaded with ornamental detail are all characteristic
of classicism which prevailed in the art of the period.

133. Samovar. 1826

In the first half of the nineteenth century samovars were executed in a variety
of forms, but the basic design was always that of a vase. Silver samovars were
lavishly ornamented with masks, dolphins, tridents with torches, vegetal scrolls
and decorative bands. The base was often adorned with openwork lattices and
provided with claw-and-ball supports. Samovars of this type were regarded
as decorative pieces and were used only on major festive occasions.

134. Doily. First quarter of the 19th century

By the beginning of the nineteenth century
various kinds of bead items had come into wide use
not only in the mansions of the gentry, but amid
the urban population as well. This octagonal miniature
doily for putting under a candlestick, with a bead fringe,
is a characteristic example of the beadwork items
of the time. The fine symmetrically arranged pattern of
roses and forget-me-nots was a frequent feature of bead
embroidery in the first half of the nineteenth century.

135, 136. Tobacco-pouch. Purses.
First half of the 19th century

Among the most popular beadwork items in
the first half of the nineteenth century were
small reticules, purses and tobacco-pouches.
Among the most favoured embroidery motifs
were floral patterns, pastoral scenes and
exotic birds. The type of decorative panel on
the blue tobacco-pouch — portraits of ladies
and officers arranged in checkerboard
fashion — was rather unusual.

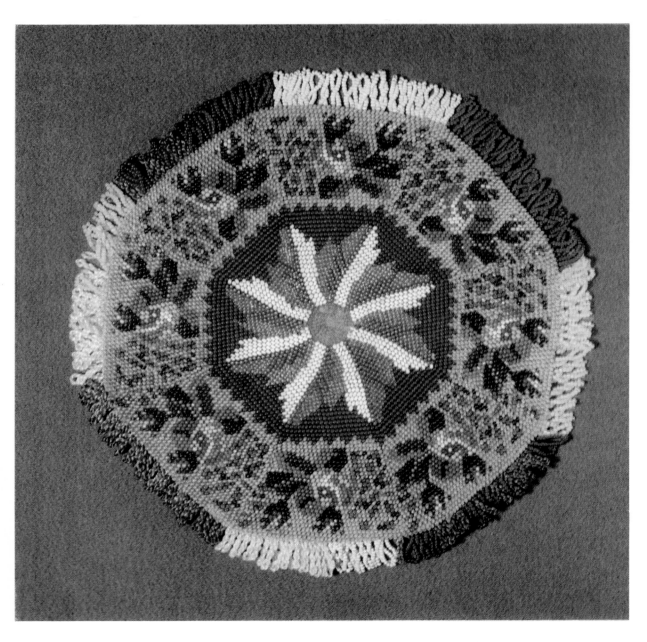

134

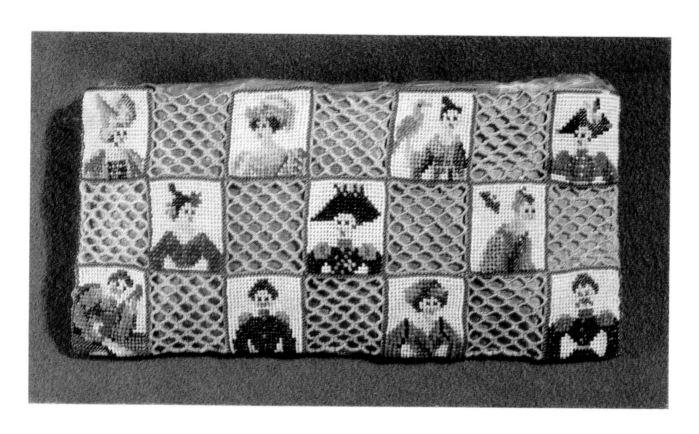

135, 136

137. Bowl. Late 18th century

Coloured glass was first obtained
in Russia by Mikhail Lomonosov, who in
1754 established the Ust-Ruditsa
factory in the environs of St. Petersburg.
The factory was the first in the country
to produce coloured glass, mosaic
smalts and beads. At the end of the
eighteenth century the production
of coloured glass was also organized
at the State factory. The bowl reproduced
is made of greenish-blue glass, a rarely
used colour. Between the golden bands
adorning the base and the rim is an
architectural landscape. Such a décor is
typical of late eighteenth century
glass objects.

138. Washing set. 1820s
The material of this washing set
is milk glass painted in blue enamel.
The bronze lid of the pitcher is
embossed and gilt. Milk glass items
with this type of decorative painting
are extremely rare.

138

139. Cups and saucers. Early 19th century

Both cups are illustrative of the type of porcelain
cup most popular in the first quarter of the
nineteenth century. One is shaped like a cylinder
with a rim bent outward, the other like
a truncated egg raised up on a round base.
The top part of each handle is raised above the
level of the body and decorated with a rosette
in relief. The decorative paintings on the cups
are enclosed in rectangular frames.
One of the paintings was done after
a miniature by F. Galaktionov (the Peterhof
fountain), the other consists of a traditional
bouquet of bright flowers in a basket.
The gilding on the saucer of the cylindrical cup
is embellished with an engraved ornament.

140

140. Tea-pot. First quarter of the 19th century
The decorative painting of the tea-pot is typical
of early nineteenth century Russian art. On the
one side is a view of the Kazan Cathedral in
St. Petersburg, on the other, the statue of Peter
the Great on Senate Square, with the building of
the Senate in the background. The miniatures are
enclosed in a rectangular frame, the rest of the
surface is gilded.

141. Vase. First half of the 19th century

The Popov Factory existed from 1811 till 1875. Four years after its foundation the press noted the superb quality of its output both in the composition of the paste and the merits of the décor. The vase depicted embodies the qualities invariably associated with this factory's wares: the effulgence of the decorative painting and the high standard of the porcelain itself.

142. Part of the service with landscapes. Late 1820s — early 1830s

In the second half of the 1820s porcelain items produced by the Gardner Factory often had the form of a truncated cone on a raised circular base. The silhouettes of these objects attained a graphic sharpness and clarity; a new device appeared in the décor: a narrow impressed band resembling a bronze hoop. The strictness of this set's forms is somewhat softened by the painted landscape with tall trees, architectural structures and tiny human figures.

143. Tray. First quarter of the 19th century

The small factory (1812—1839) owned by Batenin was famous for its decorative vases and
tableware with views of St. Petersburg and its suburbs. The painted miniatures on Batenin
porcelain were done mainly from the pictures and engravings of the better known Russian
artists of the late eighteenth and early nineteenth centuries. However, digressions from
the original were not uncommon, depending on the form of the article, the technology of
the firing and, in some instances, on the professional skill of the artisan. Other decorative
motifs favoured by Batenin's craftsmen were magnificent bouquets of flowers and
playing-card compositions. The tray reproduced presents a view of a St. Petersburg suburb.
The miniature is surrounded by an ornamental band of engraved flowers.

144. Vase. 1820s

It is believed that the vase was specially made for the first exhibition of Russian handicrafts held in St. Petersburg in 1829. The painted miniature is a view of one of the St. Petersburg theatres. The forms and décor of this largest decorative vase ever put out by the Gardner Factory are typical of Russian applied art in the first quarter of the nineteenth century. The massive handles ending in decorative lion's heads, the heavy upper part of the vessel and the graceful contours of its body are typical for the Gardner productions.

146

145. Tray. 1831

Painted on the tray is a view of the Yusupov estate in Arkhangelskoye near Moscow where a small porcelain factory was set up. N. Yusupov, who had previously headed the Imperial Porcelain Factory in St. Petersburg (1792—1802), organized production at Arkhangelskoye with the know-how born of experience. Talented serf artists were employed to decorate the plain white porcelain with painting. White porcelain ware was supplied by the Popov Factory and the Sèvres Factory in France. The subjects of the décor were miniature portraits, mythological themes and landscapes, with canvases from the rich picture gallery of Arkhangelskoye serving as the originals. Tea sets, painted dishes and cups were never meant for sale on the open market, but served as gifts to members of the Tsar's family or to friends and relatives of the Yusupovs. The Russian Museum possesses the largest number of first-class samples of the Yusupov porcelain.

146. Cup and saucer. First quarter of the 19th century

The white porcelain cup with its moulded decoration representing a cupid may have been produced in France at the Sèvres Factory. The decorative painting executed at Arkhangelskoye continues the Cupid theme and shows a lady with a cupid and a dog symbolizing love and friendship. The inner surface of the cup is covered with polished gold and the white saucer is embellished with an ornament extremely popular in the first quarter of the nineteenth century — laurel wreaths and crossed arrows.

147

147. Porcelain statuettes: "Dandy" and "Smart Lady". 1830—1840s
Among the small-size porcelain sculpture produced at the Safronov Factory most common
were statuettes representing provincial dandies and ladies of fashion. Because of their
generalized silhouette and the meticulous rendering of dress, the figurines are profoundly
expressive. Particular attention was devoted by the painter to the ornamentation,
the colour of the clothes and the décor of the work as a whole. The picturesque aspect
and humorous spirit which characterize these figurines are very much like those to be seen
in the works of folk craftsmen.

148. Porcelain figurines in theatrical costumes. 1830—1840s
Miniature porcelain statuettes of the first half of the nineteenth century often represent
men and women dressed up for a masquerade or for the stage. Details of their costumes,
such as lace and embroidery, and of the coiffures were painstakingly rendered
to imitate the real thing.

149. **Shawl.** Detail. First half of the 19th century

The monogram under the two-headed eagle indicates the shawl's place of manufacture. Founded in 1800 in the village of Skorodumovka near Nizhni Novgorod (now the city of Gorky), the Merlina Workshop was considered the first major enterprise of its kind. At the first exhibition of Russian handicrafts in St. Petersburg (1829) Merlina's shawls were awarded a gold medal. After that the trademark was changed and included, beside the monogram, a two-headed eagle and the emblem of Moscow. The shawl was evidently produced in the 1830s or 1840s.

150. **Scarf.** Detail. First quarter of the 19th century

In the first half of the nineteenth century ornamented scarves were as widely used in ladies' wear as shawls. As a rule they consisted of two strips of different colours sewn together. The pattern of beans and cucumbers, popular during the 1820s and '30s, was borrowed from the ornamental designs of the Ancient East, but its interpretation in the works of Russian women weavers was of a rather specific nature.

151, 152. Part of the dinner service of the Tver Palace. 1820s

The service consists of a large number of items and was commissioned by the Imperial office for the Tsar's palace in Tver (now the city of Kalinin), where the royal family usually stayed overnight travelling from St. Petersburg to Moscow and back. The items of the set are marked by a simplicity of form; the silhouettes are soft and graceful. The ornamentation consists of horizontal bands of flowers and leaves. The highly skilled master combines a confident brushstroke with the most delicate of lines. The painting is done in cobalt blue of many shades, from the deep and succulent to the semi-transparent, almost azurine.
The Russian Museum has in its possession over forty articles of the service which was produced at the Auerbach Factory (1812—70), one of the outstanding faience factories in Russia in the first half of the nineteenth century.

153, 154. Items from the Alexandria services. 1830s
Two services, one in crystal glass, the other
in porcelain, were commissioned for the Tsar's
summer residence, the "Alexandria" at Peterhof,
built in 1829 by the architect A. Menelas. Depicted on
all the items is a heraldic emblem — a blue shield
with a sword passing through a wreath of white roses.
The attributes of the emblem go back to the Potsdam
tournament of 1829, where the winners were crowned
with white roses for military valour. Both services
were intended for 24 diners each and included
over 5,000 items. The silhouettes and decoration of
the items reflected the Gothic taste of the designers.

155. Decanter and wine-glass. First half of the 19th century

In the 1830s a new method of decorating glass came into being — the technique of faceting two- and three-layered glass. This made it possible to create new ornamental patterns, e.g. of diamond shapes or rosettes. The vertical facets of coloured glass impart a certain shapeliness and elegance to the short, squat items.

156. Tulip-shaped glass and saucer-shaped glass. First half of the 19th century

Executed in the two-layer technique are the stems of the glasses. What makes these items especially charming is the green and ruby hue of their bodies.

156

157. Tea set. 1830—1840s
The service is characterized by a combination
of moulded decoration with painting and
gilding. The complicated form of its items
testifies to the revival of the rococo style in the
1830s and 1840s.

158. Porcelain-framed mirror. 1830—1840s
The rocaille frame with tiny moulded flowers
suggests the revival of the rococo style in
the Russian minor arts.

159. Porcelain statuette: "Esmeralda". Mid-19th century

To judge from the naiveté of this porcelain figure of Esmeralda, the Gypsy girl from Hugo's novel *Notre-Dame de Paris*, with its gaudy colours and heightened decorative quality, it was a work by an unknown master closely linked with the traditions of Ukrainian folk art. The theme was apparently suggested by the French ceramist Darte, who stood at the head of the Miklashevsky Factory. There are quite a number of works on this theme in porcelain collections. The Russian Museum's piece is noteworthy for the painter's individual approach to the décor and the treatment of detail.

161

160. Vase. Mid-19th century

The items put out by the Miklashevsky Factory
were often embellished with moulded ornament of
small brightly painted flowers. The gilded pattern
of scrolls and shells fashioned in relief is a feature
reminiscent of mid-eighteenth century porcelain; generally
speaking, porcelain objects produced a century later
were striking examples of the so-called "second rococo"
style in art.

161. Vase. Mid-19th century

In the mid-nineteenth century the technology of artistic
glass manufacture was enriched by a new process
which made possible the production of coloured
multi-layered glass. The vase reproduced
is made of two-layered glass (colourless and red).
Its elongated body with an indented rim is imitative
of the Gothic style. The painted décor is rendered
in the rococo style.

162. Wine set. 1894—96

The end of the nineteenth century witnessed a heightened interest in Russian folk art evinced by many artists. The country's silversmiths revived the old technique of enamel décor on a filigree ornament. The thin gilded strands of the filigree were intertwined into fanciful compositions of stylized flowers, birds, scrolls and geometrical figures, with the empty space filled in by multicoloured enamel to form a gay, vivid pattern. The newly aroused interest in traditional principles of design manifested itself also in the forms chosen by the artists for their items. Numerous wine bowls or loving-cups (*bratinas*), wine cups and dippers were manufactured, and by major jewellery works at that. Prominent among the latter was the Ovchinnikov Factory, especially in the production of items with enamel décor.

162

163. Vase. Mid-19th century

The forms of this vase show the influence of articles current in the countries of the east, mainly metal vessels painted in enamels.

164. Part of a coffee set. 1908—13

The décor of this coffee set for two combines a strict ornament in the style of classicism with painted genre miniatures, a feature typical of the Art Nouveau period. The elegant colour scheme, the finely drawn lines of the gilded pattern, the purity of the glaze and the paste all witness to the Imperial Porcelain Factory's traditionally high artistic culture.

165. Decorative dish "Sadko" by M. Vrubel. 1899—1900

The renowned Russian painter Mikhail Vrubel (1856—1910) has left us some interesting samples of decorative majolica. His experiments in ceramics aroused keen interest among his contemporaries and contributed to the revival in Russia of the ancient art of majolica. In 1899—1900 Vrubel created a series of sculptures, tiles and panels on Russian folk-lore themes. The motifs of the poetic bylina *Sadko* are developed in the dish reproduced, as well as in his sculpture pieces *Volkhova, Sea King* and others. The iridescent greenish-yellow and violet-blue of the glaze are harmonious with the theme of the sea, the main theme of *Sadko*. Vrubel would introduce various metal oxides into his paints which, when the item was subjected to a special firing process, produced unexpected artistic effects, so that the resulting intricate colour combinations acquired a really fantastic character. Another salient point of the dish reproduced is its large size.

168

166. Vase. 1912

Elongated shape, a blurred ornament of herbs and
flowers, a dull colour scheme — these features pertain
to the style of Art Nouveau and are all present in
glassware made in the Gallé technique. This method of
processing glass was first employed at the glass works
of Emile Gallé at Nancy, France. The glass was subjected
to etching with hydrofluoric acid, which produced an
indistinct matt ornament in relief with one hue softly
fading into another. In Russia a similar effect was
achieved in multi-layered glass objects by a complicated
process of carving.

167. "Lady with a Mask" by K. Somov. 1906

The intrinsic elegance of this work, with its
graceful, well-balanced silhouette, is
reminiscent of rococo art. The piece rates among
the finest works of early twentieth century
small-size porcelain sculpture.

168. "The Rape of Europa" by V. Serov. 1911

This sculptural group is a plastic interpretation of
V. Serov's famous water-colour of the same name.

169

169. "Head of a Lioness" by M. Vrubel. 1891
Covered by a brownish-green glaze,
this head of a lioness is marked by generalized
forms which are moulded of sharply accentuated facets.
The head was designed as an ornament for the gates
of Mamontov's house on Sadovo-Spasskaya Street
in Moscow. Vrubel's work on the architectural décor
of the Mamontov mansion illustrates the artist's quest
for a synthesis of the pictorial and decorative arts.

170. Panel. Detail. Late 19th — early 20th centuries
The ornament, which is composed of stylized flowers
and birds, and the bleached colours of this piece are
typical of the decorative fabrics of the period.

→
171. Vase. 1902
The beginning of the twentieth century
witnessed a notable change in the shapes and décor
of porcelain vases. The traditional outline, with
distinctly separated body, neck and foot, gave
place to a new silhouette. The influence of the Art
Nouveau style was also felt in the predominance
of sinuous lines forming the vegetal ornamentation.
A new technique of underglaze painting with salts,
which allowed to obtain highly picturesque effects,
came into use about the same period. One of the
prominent painters of the Imperial Porcelain Factory,
Lapshin, worked successfully in this technique.

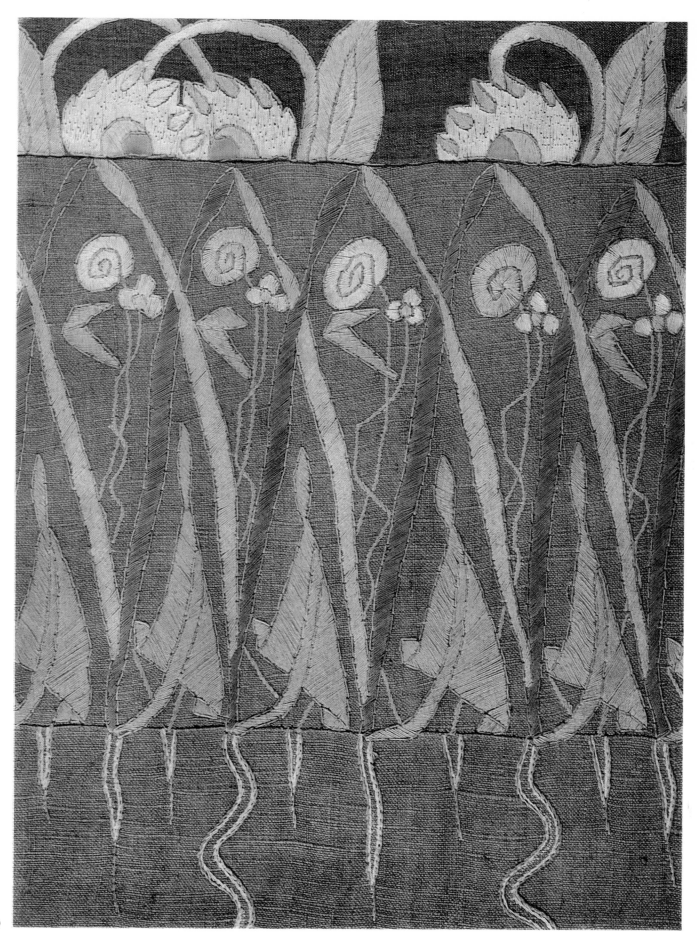

CATALOGUE

1 **Tumbler and goblet. First quarter of the 18th century**
Jamburg Glass Works
Cut glass, engraving, gilding.
Height 10.8 cm (tumbler); 20.2 cm (goblet)
Inscriptions: on the tumbler, *Виватъ царь Петеръ Алек-сеевичъ* (Vivat Tzar Peter Alexeyevich); on the goblet, *всегда счастьем* (be ever happy)
Transferred from the Hermitage in 1938
The goblet is reproduced for the first time
Inv. Nos. Ст 32, Ст 102

2, 3 **Tapestry: "The Battle of Poltava". 1723**
Imperial Tapestry Factory, St. Petersburg
By Bégagolle Jr. and I. Kobyliakov after a cartoon by L. Caravacque
Wool, metallic thread. Handwoven. 317 × 408 cm
Transferred from the Hermitage in 1935
Inv. No. Тк 1032

4 **Tapestry: "Fruit on a Table". 1717—20**
By J. Vavoque
Imperial Tapestry Factory, St. Petersburg
Silk and wool. 82 × 93 cm
Inwoven bottom right: *I·ВАВОКЪ* (Vavoque)
Received from the Hermitage in 1910
Inv. No. Тк 1059

5 **Tapestry: "Bathsheba at the Fountain". 1727**
Imperial Tapestry Factory, St. Petersburg
Silk, wool, metallic thread. 144 × 166 cm
Inwoven bottom right: *здѣлана всанктъ | питеръ | бурхѣ | дѣлалъ руско | ученикъ 1727 году* (Made in St. Petersburg, done by a Russian apprentice in 1727)
Received from the Hermitage in 1910
Inv. No. Тк 1031

6 **Gospel cover. First quarter of the 18th century**
Silver, chasing, gilding. 19.8 × 12.5 cm
Reproduced for the first time
Inv. No. Сер 31

7 **Bowl. First half of the 18th century**
Silver, niello, gilding, engraving. Height 8.5 cm
Transferred from the Hermitage in 1939
Reproduced for the first time
Inv. No. Сер 1041

8 **Tumbler with lid. 1738**
Moscow
Silver, gilding, engraving. Height 28.8 cm
Hallmarks: *738* signifying the date 1738 with the undeciphered letters *CC* under it; the emblem of Moscow with *МО...В* (part of the word Москва) under it; *iME* (unidentified hallmark)
Transferred from the Hermitage in 1939
Inv. No. Сер 1037

9 **Tea-pot. Late 1730s**
Imperial Glass Works, St. Petersburg
Coloured glass, engraving, gilding. Height 14 cm
Transferred from the Hermitage in 1938
Inv. No. Ст 43

10 **Goblet. 1740s**
St. Petersburg
Cut glass, engraving, gilding. Height 25.5 cm
Monogram: *EPI*
Transferred from the Hermitage in 1938
Reproduced for the first time
Inv. No. Ст 105

11 **Goblet. 1730s**
St. Petersburg
"Gold glass" (etched gold leaf between layers of glass). Height 22.2 cm
Monogram: *AJ*
Transferred from the Hermitage in 1938
Reproduced for the first time
Inv. No. Ст 226

12 **Goblet. Mid-18th century**
Imperial Glass Works, St. Petersburg
Cut glass, engraving, gilding. Height 24 cm
Monogram: *EP*
Transferred from the Hermitage in 1938
Reproduced for the first time
Inv. No. Ст 70

13 **Bottle. Mid-18th century**
Imperial Glass Works, St. Petersburg
Cut glass, engraving. Height 22.1 cm
Monogram: *EP*
Transferred from the Hermitage in 1927
Reproduced for the first time
Inv. No. Ст 231

14 **Book of Psalms cover.**
Second quarter of the 18th century
By Nikolai Don
Silver, paper, chasing, gilding. 20.9 × 17.5 cm
Hallmark: *НД* for Nikolai Don, silversmith, active in 1714—46
Reproduced for the first time
Inv. No. Сер 99

15 **Tureen from the Peter the Great's dinner service. Mid-18th century**
Silver, casting, chasing. Height 32 cm
Transferred from the Hermitage in 1939
Inv. No. Сер 1453

16 **Tea-kettle. 1764**
Moscow
Silver, ivory, carving, chasing, gilding. Height 77 cm

Hallmarks: the emblem of Moscow with the date *1764* under it; *BA*, the initials of an unknown tester active between 1760 and 1794
Transferred from the Hermitage in 1939
Inv. No. Сер 1344

17 Goblet. 1750s
Silver, casting, chasing. Height 16.8 cm
Hallmarks: the emblem of Moscow with the date *175[0]* under it; *ГЗ* for Gabriel Sonntag, silversmith, active between 1747 and 1780; *АГ* for Andrei Gerasimov, silversmith, active between 1739 and 1763
Reproduced for the first time
Inv. No. Сер 1010

18 Tapestry: "Wild Animals Fighting at a Watering-place". 1747
Imperial Tapestry Factory, St. Petersburg
Silk, wool. 310 × 280 cm
Monogram: *EP*
Inwoven bottom right: *всанктпѣтербургѣ. 1747. году*
(Done in St. Petersburg in 1747)
Transferred from the Hermitage in 1938
Inv. No. Тк 1026

19 Side-table and candelabrum. Mid-18th century
Wood, carving, gilding, painting. 150 × 92 × 57 cm
Acquired in 1920s
Reproduced for the first time
Inv. No. Меб 670

20 Mirror. Mid-18th century
Glass, wood, carving, gilding. 117 × 60 cm
Acquired in 1957
Reproduced for the first time
Inv. No. Меб 981

21 "Chair" tapestry. 1750s
Imperial Tapestry Factory, St. Petersburg
Silk, wool. 74 × 76 cm
Received from the Hermitage in 1910
Inv. No. Тк 1060

22, 23 Bureau bookcase. 1740—1750s
Wood, carving, gilding, painting in oil.
242 × 115 × 61 cm
Transferred from the Chinese Palace in Oranienbaum in 1918
Inv. No. Меб 798

24 Mirror. Second half of the 18th century
Glass, wood, carving, gilding. 148 × 59 cm
Reproduced for the first time
Inv. No. Меб 574

25 Candelabrum. Mid-18th century
Cut glass, ormolu. Height 81.8 cm
Received from the State Museum Reserve in 1922
Inv. No. Ст 2081

26 Snuff-box. Second half of the 18th century
Imperial Porcelain Factory, St. Petersburg
Porcelain, overglaze painting, gilding. Gold mount.
6 × 12 × 10.7 cm
Acquired in 1974
Inv. No. Сер 1141

27 Biscuit-dish. Early 1760s
Imperial Porcelain Factory, St. Petersburg
Porcelain, overglaze painting. Height 12.6 cm
Mark in gold: a two-headed eagle
Transferred from the Hermitage in 1932
Inv. No. Ф 408

28 Special bowl for wine-glasses. 1750s
Imperial Porcelain Factory, St. Petersburg
Porcelain, overglaze painting, gilding. 12 × 25.1 × 18.4 cm
Acquired in 1932
Reproduced for the first time
Inv. No. Ф 553

29 Scent vase. Late 1750s
Imperial Porcelain Factory, St. Petersburg
Porcelain, overglaze painting, gilding. Height 33.8 cm
Mark in underglaze blue: a two-headed eagle
Transferred from the Hermitage in 1932
Inv. No. Ф 501

30, 31 Part of Her Majesty's Private Service. Late 1750s
Imperial Porcelain Factory, St. Petersburg
Porcelain, overglaze painting, gilding. Diam. 24 cm (plate); height 13.8 cm (tureen); length of the spoons, 19.1 cm, 21.7 cm
Mark in overglaze black: a two-headed eagle
Transferred from the Hermitage in 1932
Inv. Nos. Ф 423, Ф 459, Ф 420, Ф 407

32, 33 Items from the Orlov service. Early 1760s
Imperial Porcelain Factory, St. Petersburg
Porcelain, overglaze and underglaze painting, gilding.
Diam. 24 cm (plate), 12.7 cm (saucer); length 24.3 cm (knife-handle), 18.6 cm (spoon); height 13.8 cm (tea-pot). 5 cm (cup)
Monogram: *ГГО*
Impressed in the paste: a two-headed eagle (tea-pot and cup); mark in overglaze black: a two-headed eagle; in gold: *N° 1*
Transferred from the Hermitage in 1932
Inv. Nos. Ф 578, Ф 590, Ф 591, Ф 577, Ф 575

34 Perfume vase. 1780
Imperial Porcelain Factory, St. Petersburg
Porcelain, overglaze painting, gilding. 51 × 14 cm
Inscribed: *1780*
Mark in underglaze blue: *E II*
Inv. No. Ф 311

35 Desk. 1779
J. G. Kohl's workshop, St. Petersburg
Veneered mahogany inlaid with ivory, brass and bronze.
116 × 110 × 58.5 cm
Inscription: *St: Petersburg den. 23.*
Februa[r] Anno 1.7.7.9. JG Kohl
Acquired in 1965
Reproduced for the first time
Inv. No. Меб 1010

36 Tapestry: "Venus Riding Dolphins". 1763
By Master Fedot
Imperial Tapestry Factory, St. Petersburg
Silk, wool. Handwoven. 109 × 84 cm
Monogram: *EA II*
Inwoven bottom right: *:ВС·П·Б·ткалъБаслист · / Ундер-Мастер· / Θедот· / 1763:·* (Woven in basse-lisse in St. Petersburg by junior master Fedot 1763)
Acquired in 1966
Inv. No. Тк 1669

37, 38 Candelabra. Late 18th century
Cut glass, ormolu, marble.
Height 93.5 cm (left); 90 cm (right)
Received from the State Museum Reserve in 1932 (inv. No. Ст 2078), and from a private collection (inv. No. Ст 1631)
Reproduced for the first time

39 Panel: "Picnic". Second half of the 18th century
Beadwork, bugles and decorative oil painting on canvas.
51 × 79 cm
Transferred from the Museum of the History of Leningrad in 1932
Inv. No. Ст 2345

40 Panel: "Prometheus".
Second half of the 18th century
Buglework on canvas. 98 × 98 cm
Inv. No. Ст 2346

41 Dish. Second half of the 18th century
Gzhel, Moscow province
Majolica, overglaze painting. Diam. 28.5 cm
Transferred from the Hermitage in 1938
Reproduced for the first time
Inv. No. Фс 461

42 Tea-caddy. Second half of the 18th century
Copper, stamped silver, enamel. Height 11 cm
Transferred from the Hermitage in 1939
Reproduced for the first time
Inv. No. Ст 2491

43, 44 Tiles. Second half of the 18th century
Clay, enamelled and glazed. 22 × 18 cm (each tile)
Acquired in 1900
Reproduced for the first time
Inv. Nos. Фс 789—795

45 Tray. Second half of the 18th century
The Popovs' Factory, Veliky Ustiug
Copper, enamel, silver. 34 × 25.9 cm
Transferred from the History Department of the Russian Museum in 1934
Reproduced for the first time
Inv. No. Ст 2456

46 Coffee-pot and tea-pot. 1780
The Popovs' Factory, Veliky Ustiug
Copper, enamel, silver. Height 19.5 cm (coffee-pot), 9.3 cm (tea-pot)
Monogram: *MRG*; date: *1780*
Transferred from the Hermitage in 1938
Reproduced for the first time
Inv. Nos. Ст 2447, Ст 2448

47 Tureen. Second half of the 18th century
Imperial Porcelain Factory, St. Petersburg
Porcelain, overglaze painting. Height 25.2 cm
Mark in underglaze blue: *E II*
Transferred from the Hermitage in 1932
Reproduced for the first time
Inv. No. Ф 194

48 Kvass jar. Second half of the 18th century
Imperial Porcelain Factory, St. Petersburg
Porcelain, overglaze painting. Height 34.8 cm
Mark in overglaze green: *E II*
Transferred from the Hermitage in 1932
Reproduced for the first time
Inv. No. Ф 855

49—53 Items from the Arabesque service. 1784
Imperial Porcelain Factory, St. Petersburg
Transferred from the Hermitage in 1932
Plate, ice-cream pail, bowl for wine-glasses
Porcelain, overglaze painting, gilding. Diam. 24 cm (plate); height 21.7 cm (ice-cream pail); 12.3 × 18.2 × 29.5 cm (bowl for wine-glasses)
Mark in underglaze blue: *E II*
Inv. Nos. Ф 1035, Ф 1047, Ф 1176
Decorative pieces: "Allegory of Justice", "Allegory of Sea Power"
After models by Jean-Dominique Rachette
Porcelain, ormolu. Height 24.9 cm (*Justice*); 52 cm (*Sea Power*)
Monogram: *E II* under the Imperial crown (*Justice*)
Inv. Nos. Ф 687, Ф 692

54, 56 Tureen and plate from the Yacht service.
1780—1790s
Imperial Porcelain Factory, St. Petersburg
Porcelain, overglaze painting, gilding.
Height 29.5 cm (tureen); diam. 24.5 cm (plate)
Mark in underglaze blue: *E II*
Transferred from the Hermitage in 1932
Inv. Nos. Ф 1222, Ф 1313

55 Part of the Yacht service. 1780—1790s

Imperial Porcelain Factory, St. Petersburg
Porcelain, overglaze painting, gilding. Height 29.5 cm
(tureen), 10 cm (mustard-pot), 9.6 cm (salt-cellar)
Mark in underglaze blue: *E II*
Transferred from the Hermitage in 1932
Inv. Nos. Ф 1317, Ф 1303, Ф 1300

**57, 58 Porcelain statuettes: "Estonian Peasant Woman",
"Kazan Tartar", "Bagpiper Boy", "Peasant Girl Selling Berries". Second half of the 18th century**

Imperial Porcelain Factory, St. Petersburg
Porcelain, overglaze painting.
Height 22 cm, 22 cm, 17 cm, 20.2 cm
Transferred from the Hermitage in 1932
Inv. Nos. Ф 635, Ф 659, Ф 666, Ф 636

59, 60 Jug. Sugar-basin. Second half of the 18th century

Milk glass, polychrome painting.
Height 24.8 cm (jug), 14.3 cm (sugar-basin)
Transferred from the Hermitage in 1938
Sugar-basin reproduced for the first time
Inv. Nos. Ст 280, Ст 278

61 Goblet. Mid-18th century

Cut glass, engraving. 36.7 × 16 cm
Monogram: *АГГ* and inscription: *Здравие его сиятелства
действителнаго тайнаго советника ордена светаго апостала
Андрея ковалера чрезвычайнаго полномочнаго посла и ми-
нистра графа Александра Гавриловича Головкина намно-
гая лета многая лета многая лета* (To the health of
Count Alexander Gavrilovich Golovkin, Privy Councillor,
Knight of the Order of St. Andrew, Ambassador Pleni-
potentiary and Minister of State, for many, many years)
Transferred from the Hermitage in 1938
Reproduced for the first time
Inv. No. Ст 1622

62 Goblet. Second half of the 18th century

Cut glass, engraving. Height 25 cm
Transferred from the Hermitage in 1938
Reproduced for the first time
Inv. No. C 195

63 Kvasnik (kvass bowl). Late 18th century

Glass, polychrome painting, gilding. Height 25 cm
Transferred from the Hermitage in 1938
Inv. No. Ст 593

64 Bowl. Late 18th century

Glass, gilding. Height (with lid) 20 cm
Transferred from the Pavlovsk Palace in 1932
Reproduced for the first time
Inv. No. Ст 362

**65 Part of a set for wine and fruit.
Late 18th century**

Cut glass, gilding. Height 28.5 cm (decanter),
9.4 cm (wine-glass)
Monogram: *AO*
Transferred from the Historical Department
of the Russian Museum in 1934
Inv. Nos. Ст 564, Ст 570

66 Wine-glasses. Late 18th century

Coloured glass, painting in gold. Height 11.8 cm, 10.5 cm
Monograms: *П I* under the Imperial crown (left glass);
CX, *MX* (right glass)
Transferred from the Hermitage in 1938 (left glass)
and from the History Department of the Russian Museum
in 1934 (right glass)
The ruby wine glass is reproduced for the first time
Inv. Nos. Ст 361, Ст 359

67 Toilet mirror. 18th century

Glass, wood, carved ivory. 81 × 54 × 19 cm
Acquired in 1928
Reproduced for the first time
Inv. No. P 269

68 Cup. Second half of the 18th century

Carved ivory. Height 20.8 cm
Inscription: *Ни того нидругаго небоится* (afraid of neither
one nor the other)
Transferred from the History Department of the Russian
Museum in 1934
Reproduced for the first time
Inv. No. P 190

**69 Panel with portraits.
Second half of the 18th century**

Ivory, wood. 20.3 × 16 cm
Inscription: *В·кн·Павелъ·Петровичъ·в·кн·Мария·
Ѳеодоровн[а]* (Grand Prince Pavel Petrovich, Grand
Princess Maria Feodorovna)
Transferred from the Sculpture Department of the
Russian Museum in 1952
Reproduced for the first time
Inv. No. P 142

70 Casket. Second half of the 18th century

Ivory, wood, cloth, metal, carving. 11.5 × 11 × 9 cm
Acquired in 1968
Reproduced for the first time
Inv. No. P 394

**71, 72 Bean-shaped table.
Second half of the 18th century**

Inlaid wood, brass. 96 × 76 × 50 cm
Transferred from the Museum of the October
Revolution in 1934
Reproduced for the first time
Inv. No. Меб 669

73—75 Desk. 1770s

Inlaid wood. 102 × 95 × 60 cm
Transferred from the Hermitage in 1932
Inv. No. Меб 570

**76, 77 Art objects in steel.
Late 18th century**

Arms Factory, Tula
Reproduced for the first time
Mirror
Steel, glass. 28 × 36 × 30 cm
Transferred from the Hermitage in 1932
Inv. No. M 194
Candlestick
Steel. Height 34 cm
Received from the State Museum Reserve in 1931
Inv. No. M 202
Casket
By I. Svechnikov
Steel. 4 × 9.6 × 6.9 cm
Inscribed on lid: *Въ Тулѣ И. Свечниковъ* (In Tula.
I. Svechnikov)
Acquired in 1971
Inv. No. M 609
Inkstand
Steel. 16.5 × 21.5 × 13 cm
Transferred from the Artistic Handicrafts Department
of the Russian Museum in 1938
Reproduced for the first time
Inv. No. M 210

78 Potir. 1794

Silver, niello, gilding. 34 × 12.5 cm
Hallmarks: emblem of Moscow with the date *1794* under
it; *AB*, the initials of an unidentified master, active
1793—94; *МЦС*, the initials of another unidentified
master, active 1793—94
Transferred from the Astoria Hotel, Leningrad, in 1936
Inv. No. Сер 115

79 Gospel cover. 1775

Silver, chasing, gilding. 48.5 × 33.5 cm
Hallmarks: emblem of St. Petersburg above the date *1775*;
ЗД for Zacharius Deichman, silversmith; *НМ* for Nikifor
Moshchalkin and *ИѲ* for Ivan Frolov, testers
Received from the State Museum Reserve in 1937
Reproduced for the first time
Inv. No. Сер 14

80 Snuff-box. Late 18th century

Veliky Ustiug
Silver, niello, engraving, gilding. 1.8 × 8.6 cm
Inscriptions: *Карта Вологодской губерніи; в дюймѣ 364 ес
52 156 200; всего мерою окружной межы 4249 верстъ*
(map of Vologda province with indications of scale)
Hallmarks: *ѲБ* for Fiodor Bushkovsky, active 1795—1834;
AT for Alexei Torlov, active 1768—1809; emblem of Ve-
liky Ustiug (the sign of Aquarius)

Received from the State Museum Reserve in 1937
Inv. No. Сер 1099

81 Tea-pot. Second half of the 18th century

Silver, niello, engraving, gilding. 12.9 × 14.3 × 8.4 cm
Transferred from the Hermitage in 1939
Reproduced for the first time
Inv. No. Сер 1439

82 Flask. 1774

Silver, niello. Height 17.7 cm
Monogram: *ДЧ* and the coat-of-arms of the Chicherin
family
Hallmarks: emblem of Siberia current between 1765 and
1780; *МПШ*, the initials of an unidentified master who
worked in Tobolsk in 1774—80; under the date *1774* the
initials *ЛВ* for the tester Lev Vlasov, also active in
Tobolsk in 1757—80
Transferred from the Hermitage in 1939
Reproduced for the first time
Inv. No. Сер 1361

83 Tankard and cup. Mid-18th century

The Demidov works, Urals
Brass, chasing. Height 20.5 cm (tankard), 7 cm (cup)
Hallmarks: on the tankard, the letters *МОФ, УСФ, МВП*
above the date *1751*
Transferred from the Hermitage in 1938
Inv. Nos. M 54, M 311

84 Samovar. Late 18th century

By N. and G. Chernikov
Patinated brass, engraving, chasing. Height 34.4 cm
Engraved on lid: *ВТулѣ Н. Г. Черниковы*
Acquired in 1968
Inv. No. M 559

85 Kvasnik. Second half of the 18th century

Imperial Porcelain Factory, St. Petersburg
Porcelain, overglaze painting, gilding. 21.9 × 17.5 × 12 cm
Monogram: *AB*. Mark in underglaze blue: *E II*
Reproduced for the first time
Inv. No. Ф 905

**86 Part of the service with views of
the Pavlovsk park. Late 1790s**

Imperial Porcelain Factory, St. Petersburg
Porcelain, overglaze and underglaze painting, gilding.
Diam. 36.2 cm (tray), 13.9 cm (saucer); height 19.6 cm
(coffee-pot), 9.6 cm (sugar-basin), 9.8 cm (cup)
Mark in underglaze blue: the Russian Imperial crown and
the letter *П*. Monogram: *M*
Transferred from the Hermitage in 1932 (the tray in 1938)
Inv. Nos. Ф 1620, Ф 1618, Ф 1622, Ф 1616

87 Tea-pot. Second half of the 18th century

The Gardner Factory, Moscow province
Porcelain, overglaze painting, gilding. Height 16 cm
Acquired in 1933
Inv. No. Ф 6581

88 Part of a tea set. 1775

The Gardner Factory, Moscow province
Painted by J. Kaestner
Porcelain, overglaze painting, gilding.
Diam. 32.2 cm (tray); height 8.9 cm (tea-pot), 4.1 cm
(cup), 9.8 cm (creamer)
Monogram: *E II*
Inscription in gold on tray: *J. C. Kaestner. inv. et
fecit 1775.*
Mark in underglaze blue: *I*
Transferred from the Hermitage in 1932
Inv. Nos. Ф 6133—6136

89 Part of the St. Andrew dinner service. 1777—80

The Gardner Factory, Moscow province
Porcelain, overglaze painting, gilding. Diam. 25 cm
(plate); height 10.2 cm (creamer), 4.8 cm (salt-cellar);
length 9.8 cm (knife-handle)
Inscription on plate: *завѣру·ивѣрностъ* (for faith
and loyalty)
Mark in underglaze blue: *С*
Transferred from the Hermitage in 1927 (creamer), in 1932
(plate and salt-cellar), in 1938 (knife-handle)
Inv. Nos. Ф 6016, Ф 6057, Ф 6047, Ф 6075

**90 Part of the St. Alexander Nevsky dinner service.
1777—80**

The Gardner Factory, Moscow province
Porcelain, overglaze painting, gilding. Diam. 23.5 cm
(plate); height 9.7 cm (creamer), 4.2 cm (salt-cellar)
Inscription: *затрудъ·іотечество* (for labour and Fatherland)
Mark in underglaze blue: *С*
Transferred from the Hermitage in 1932
Inv. Nos. Ф 6196, Ф 6238, Ф 6244

**91 Part of the St. Alexander Nevsky dinner service.
1777—80**

The Gardner Factory, Moscow province
Porcelain, overglaze painting, gilding. Diam. 30.6 cm,
18.7 cm (dishes); length 9.2 cm, 8.6 cm (knife-handles)
Inscription: *затрудъ·іотечество* (for labour and
Fatherland)
Mark in underglaze blue: *С*
Transferred from the Hermitage in 1932
Inv. Nos. Ф 6226, Ф 6231, Ф 6256, Ф 6261

92 Coffee set. Late 18th century

Imperial Porcelain Factory, St. Petersburg
Porcelain, underglaze painting, gilding. Diam. 28.5 cm
(tray), 12.6 cm (saucer); height 14.5 cm (coffee-pot),
10.9 cm (creamer), 9.4 cm (cup)
Marks in underglaze blue: *E II* (tray, coffee-pot),
II (saucer), A_I (creamer)
Transferred from the Hermitage in 1932 (coffee-pot
in 1938)
Inv. Nos. Ф 1549, Ф 1520, Ф 1553, Ф 1551

**93 Bowl for wine-glasses from the Cabinet service.
Late 1790s**

Imperial Porcelain Factory, St. Petersburg
Porcelain, overglaze painting, gilding. 12 × 19 × 31.2 cm
Inscription on the base in black: *Vüe pris dans les environs
de Leon Fort; vüe pris a Casiro Giovani, l'antique
ville d'Enna* [sic]
Mark in underglaze blue: the Russian Imperial crown
and the letter *II*
Transferred from the Hermitage in 1932
Inv. No. Ф 1766

94 Vase. Late 18th — first third of the 19th century

Imperial Porcelain Factory, St. Petersburg
Porcelain, overglaze painting, gilding. Height 46 cm
Received from the State Museum Reserve in 1922
Reproduced for the first time
Inv. No. Ф 1671

95 Vase. Early 19th century

Coloured and milk glass, polychrome painting.
Height 52 cm
Transferred from the Hermitage in 1939
Reproduced for the first time
Inv. No. Ст 2077

96 Egg-shaped vase. 1796—1801

Imperial Porcelain Factory, St. Petersburg
Porcelain, ormolu, marble; overglaze and underglaze
painting. Height 66 cm
Monogram of Paul I in gold
Transferred from the Hermitage in 1932
Inv. No. Ф 1675

97 Toilet table. Late 18th century

Veneered mahogany. 164 × 110.5 × 58 cm
Received in 1955
Reproduced for the first time
Inv. No. Меб 928

98 Candelabrum. Late 18th century

Cut glass, ormolu. 79 × 55 cm
Reproduced for the first time
Inv. No. М 433

99 Vase. Late 18th century

Wood, carving, gilding. Height 69 cm
Acquired in 1958
Reproduced for the first time
Inv. No. Д 221

**100 Tapestry: "Telemachus Recounting His Exploit to
Calypso". Detail. Second half of the 18th century**

Wool, silk, gold thread. 263 × 238 cm
Inwoven caption: *Теле / макъ росказы / ваетъ*

свие | похожъде | ние Кали | пъсъ (Telemachus recounting his exploit to Calypso)
Inv. No. Тк 1064

101   Bracket. Late 18th century

Carved wood, gilding. 73 × 45 × 25 cm
Received from the State Museum Reserve in 1937
Reproduced for the first time
Inv. No. Д 142

102   Clock. Late 18th century

Carved wood, copper, gilding. 77 × 60 × 21 cm
Transferred from the Museum of the History of Leningrad in 1932
Reproduced for the first time
Inv. No. Д 99

**103   Cloth. Fragment of a chasuble.
Late 18th century**

Silk, brocade thread
Received from Tikhvin in 1932
Reproduced for the first time
Inv. No. Тк 134

104   Vase. Early 19th century

By A. Voronikhin (?)
Lapidary Works, Ekaterinburg
Serpentine stone. 56 × 66 cm
Transferred from the Yelagin Palace in 1930
Inv. No. Р 292

**105   Embroidery. Fragment of a chasuble.
Late 18th century**

Silk, gold thread
Received from the State Museum Reserve in 1932
Inv. No. Тк 285

106   Cloth. Fragment of a cope. Late 18th century

Silk, brocade thread
Received from Tikhvin in 1932
Reproduced for the first time
Inv. No. Тк 90

107   Vase. First quarter of the 19th century

Flint glass, ormolu. Height 61 cm
Acquired in 1965
Reproduced for the first time
Inv. No. Ст 3209

**108   Toilet table and mirror.
First quarter of the 19th century**

Designed by Rossi
Cast silver, cast bronze, crystal glass, smalt; gilding, chasing. 81 × 144 × 87 cm (table); 83.5 × 103 × 22 cm (mirror)
Received from the Oranienbaum Palace in 1927 (table) and in 1917 (mirror)
Inv. Nos. Меб 391, Меб 178

109   Vase. First quarter of the 19th century

Imperial Porcelain Factory, St. Petersburg
Porcelain, ormolu, overglaze painting, gilding.
Height 69 cm
Monogram: A_I under the Imperial crown
Reproduced for the first time
Inv. No. Ф 4424

110   Settee. First quarter of the 19th century

Veneered mahogany, carving, painting, gilding.
190 × 145 × 66 cm
Reproduced for the first time
Inv. No. Меб 677

111   Chair. First quarter of the 19th century

Painted wood, carving, gilding. 88 × 51 × 49 cm
Reproduced for the first time
Inv. No. Меб 619

112   Chair. Early 19th century

Wood, carving, gilding. 98.9 × 58 × 57 cm
Transferred from the Hermitage in 1932
Reproduced for the first time
Inv. No. Меб 448

113   Carpet. First quarter of the 19th century

Imperial Tapestry Factory, St. Petersburg
Wool. Handwoven. 415 × 442 cm
Transferred from the Yelagin Palace (Leningrad) in the 1930s
Inv. No. Тк 1022

114   Vase. 1819

Painted by K. Adams
Imperial Porcelain Factory, St. Petersburg
Porcelain, overglaze painting, gilding. Height 108 cm
Signed: *K. Adams*
Reproduced for the first time
Inv. No. Ф 4426

115—119   Part of the Guryev service. 1809

Imperial Porcelain Factory, St. Petersburg
Porcelain, overglaze painting, gilding. 20 × 23.6 × 20.2 cm (ice-pail); diam. 25.3 cm, 25.2 cm, 25 cm (plates); height 24 cm (tazza)
Inscriptions: pl. 116, *разнощик съ куличами* (pedlar with Easter cakes); pl. 117, *игра въ свайку* (the "svaika" game); pl. 119, *показывают тюленя* (showing a seal)
Transferred from Peterhof in 1927 (tazza and ice-pail), from the Hermitage in 1932 (plates)
Reproduced for the first time
Inv. Nos. Ф 2418, Ф 2336, Ф 2416, Ф 2330, Ф 2327

120   Part of the Green service. 1830s

Imperial Porcelain Factory, St. Petersburg
Porcelain, overglaze painting, gilding and engraving.
Height 18 cm (tea-pot), 9.9 cm (cup), 15.2 cm (sugar-bowl); diam. 54 cm (tray), 15.5 cm (saucer)
Transferred from the Hermitage in 1932
Inv. Nos. Ф 2954, Ф 2958, Ф 2956, Ф 2961

121 Cup and saucer. First quarter of the 19th century

Imperial Porcelain Factory, St. Petersburg
Porcelain, overglaze painting, gilding.
Height 10.5 cm (cup); diam. 17.4 cm (saucer)
Acquired in 1965 through the Purchasing Commission of
Experts
Reproduced for the first time
Inv. No. Ф 9540

**122, 123 Tumbler and two goblets.
First quarter of the 19th century**

Cut glass, gilding, sepia and polychrome painting.
Height 12 cm (tumbler), 18.9 cm (each goblet)
Inscriptions: on the tumbler, *Графъ Платовъ* (Count
Platov); on the goblets, *Графъ Витгенштейнъ* (Count
Wittgenstein), *Князь Кутузовъ Смоленскій*
(Prince Kutuzov Smolensky)
Received from the State Museum Reserve in 1928
Inv. Nos. Ст 429, Ст 455, Ст 431

**124 Articles of malachite.
First half of the 19th century**

Lapidary Works, Ekaterinburg
Toilet set
Malachite, ormolu, cut glass. Height 34 cm
Inv. No. M 317
Paper-weight
Malachite, bronze. 7 × 12.5 cm
Inv. No. M 332
Table ornament
Malachite, ormolu. 13 × 17.5 cm
Inv. No. M 323

Transferred from the Hermitage in 1938
Reproduced for the first time

125 Candelabrum. First half of the 19th century

Cut glass, ormolu. 96 × 34.7 cm
Inv. No. Ст 1626

126 Clock case. 1849

Kiev-Mezhigorye Factory
Faience. 22 × 12.2 × 7.9 cm
Impressed in the paste: *Кiев 1849 октября*
(Kiev, 1849, October)
Acquired in 1960 through the Purchasing Commission
of Experts
Reproduced for the first time
Inv. No. Фс 1357

127 Cloth. First half of the 19th century

Silk, cotton thread. 61 × 109 cm
Transferred from the Hermitage in 1938
Reproduced for the first time
Inv. No. Тк 753

128 Kerchief. First half of the 19th century

The Levin Silk-weaving Mill, Kolomna, Moscow province
Silk, gold thread. 108 × 110 cm
Inwoven in green along the border: *С. Ш. Ф. К. К. В.
Л. С. Л.*
Transferred from the Hermitage in 1938
Reproduced for the first time
Inv. No. Тк 35

**129 "Girl with a Pitcher".
First quarter of the 19th century**

Imperial Porcelain Factory, St. Petersburg
Porcelain, overglaze painting. Height 21.4 cm
Impressed in the paste: *118*
Acquired in 1946
Reproduced for the first time
Inv. No. Ф 2302

130 "Peasant Lad". 1810s

Imperial Porcelain Factory, St. Petersburg
Porcelain, biscuit (glazed in places), overglaze painting.
Height 26.6 cm
Impressed in the paste: *12*
Transferred from the Hermitage in 1938
Inv. No. Ф 2300

131 Dish. 1810—1820s

The Novy Brothers' Factory, Moscow province
Faience, overglaze painting. Diam. 25 cm
Impressed in the paste: *Ivan Novai*
Transferred from the Hermitage in 1938
Reproduced for the first time
Inv. No. Фс 85

132 Tankard. 1835

Rolled and stamped silver. Height (with lid) 8.1 cm
Hallmarks: the emblem of Moscow with the date *1835*
under it; *84* for the standard; *ВА*, the initials of
an unidentified master; *НД* for Nikolai Dubrovin, tester,
active 1822—55
Acquired in 1965
Reproduced for the first time
Inv. No. Сер 2034

133 Samovar. 1826

Chased silver, wood, gilding. Height 46.8 cm
Hallmarks: *МГ* for the unidentified master of the first
half of the 19th century; above the date, *1826*, the
initials *Н. Д.* for the tester Nikolai Dubrovin, active
1822—55; *84* for the standard; the emblem of Moscow
Acquired in 1969
Inv. No. Сер 2060

134 Doily. First quarter of the 19th century

Beadwork on linen. 12.5 × 12.5 cm
Acquired in 1939
Reproduced for the first time
Inv. No. Ст 2111

**135, 136 Tobacco-pouch and purses.
First half of the 19th century**

Silk tobacco-pouch with beadwork panel
Silk, beadwork on linen. 17 × 25 cm
Transferred from the Hermitage in 1938
Inv. No. Ст 2909

Purse with girl and lamb
Beadwork on linen. 8.5 × 12 cm
Acquired in 1939
Inv. No. Ст 2116

Purse with parrot
Beadwork on linen. 8.5 × 11 cm
Inv. No. Ст 3026

Reproduced for the first time

137 Bowl. Late 18th century

St. Petersburg
Glass, painting in sepia, gilding. Height 11.8 cm
Acquired in 1932
Reproduced for the first time
Inv. No. Ст 994

138 Washing set. 1820s

Glass, bronze, painting, embossing, gilding.
Height 32.3 cm (pitcher); diam. 37 cm (basin)
Monogram: *EM*
Transferred from the Hermitage in 1938
Reproduced for the first time
Inv. Nos. Ст 688, Ст 689

139 Cups and saucers. Early 19th century

The Gardner Factory, Moscow province
Porcelain, overglaze painting, engraving. Left: height
9.7 cm (cup), diam. 13 cm (saucer); right: height 13.8 cm
(cup), diam. 13.8 (saucer)
Mark in underglaze blue: *G*
Acquired in 1961 through the Purchasing Commission of
Experts
Reproduced for the first time
Inv. Nos. Ф 6898, Ф 9447

140 Tea-pot. First quarter of the 19th century

The Batenin Factory, St. Petersburg
Porcelain, overglaze painting, gilding. Height 20.5 cm
Impressed in the paste: *С. ЗКБ*
Acquired in 1964 through the Purchasing Commission of
Experts
Reproduced for the first time
Inv. No. Ф 9495

141 Vase. First half of the 19th century

The Popov Factory, Moscow province
Porcelain, overglaze painting, gilding. Height 45 cm
Mark in underglaze blue: *АП*
Transferred from the Hermitage in 1937
Reproduced for the first time
Inv. No. Ф 7434

**142 Part of the service with landscapes.
Late 1820s — early 1830s**

The Gardner Factory, Moscow province
Porcelain, overglaze painting, gilding.
Height 25.5 cm (coffee-pot), 15.2 cm (creamer), 9.4 cm
(cups); diam. 14.7 cm (saucer)
Marks in underglaze blue: *G*, in black: $\frac{№\ 1}{19}$, impressed in
the paste: *Гарднеръ 2* (coffee-pot, tea-pot); in gold: *G*,
in purple: $\frac{№\ 2}{106}$, impressed in the paste: the emblem of
Moscow, *Гарднеръ 10* (cup); in gold: *G*, in purple: $\frac{№\ 2}{2}$,
impressed in the paste: the emblem of Moscow, *Гарднеръ 10*
(saucer).
Transferred from the History Department of the Russian
Museum in 1935 (creamer); received from the State
Museum Reserve in 1937 (other items)
Reproduced for the first time
Inv. Nos. Ф 7041, Ф 7038, Ф 7039

143 Tray. First quarter of the 19th century

The Batenin Factory, St. Petersburg
Porcelain, overglaze and underglaze painting, engraving,
gilding. 27.7 × 27.5 cm
Transferred from the former Shuvalov Palace,
St. Petersburg, in 1925
Reproduced for the first time
Inv. No. Ф 9228

144 Vase. 1820s

The Gardner Factory, Moscow province
Porcelain, overglaze painting, gilding. Height 73.5 cm
Mark in underglaze blue: *G*; impressed in the paste:
гарднеръ
Acquired in 1958
Reproduced for the first time
Inv. No. Ф 9368

145 Tray. 1831

The Yusupov Factory, Moscow province
Porcelain, overglaze painting and gilding. 31 × 23 cm
Mark in underglaze blue: *А II*; date in overglaze red: *1831*
Transferred from the Hermitage in 1932
Reproduced for the first time
Inv. No. В 8836

146 Cup and saucer. First quarter of the 19th century

The Yusupov Factory, Moscow province
Porcelain, overglaze painting, gilding, moulded decoration.
Height 9 cm (cup); diam. 17.8 cm (saucer)
Received from the State Museum Reserve in 1941
Inv. No. Ф 8784

147 "Dandy" and "Smart Lady". 1830—1840s

The Safronov Factory, Moscow province
Porcelain, overglaze painting, gilding.
Height 17.5 cm, 18.8 cm
Mark in underglaze blue: *C*

Acquired through the Purchasing Commission of Experts in 1958 (*Smart Lady*) and 1966 (*Dandy*)
Reproduced for the first time
Inv. Nos. Ф 9569, Ф 9379

148 Figurines in theatrical costumes. 1830—1840s

Imperial Porcelain Factory, St. Petersburg
Porcelain, overglaze painting, gilding.
Height 14.2 cm, 14.8 cm
Mark in underglaze blue: H_I
Transferred from the Hermitage in 1938; acquired from a private collection in 1964
Reproduced for the first time
Inv. Nos. Ф 3348, Ф 9514

149 Shawl. First half of the 19th century. Detail

The N. Merlina Workshop, Nizhni Novgorod province
Goat's down, silk thread. Handwoven. 160 × 160 cm
Monogram in border: *H: M:*
Acquired in 1946
Reproduced for the first time
Inv. No. Тк 862

150 Scarf. First half of the 19th century. Detail

Goat's down, silk thread. Handwoven. 50 × 226 cm
Acquired in 1946
Reproduced for the first time
Inv. No. Тк 866

151, 152 Part of the dinner service from the Tver Palace. 1820s

The Auerbach Factory, Tver province
Faience, underglaze painting. Height 27 cm (tureen), 22.4 cm (coffee-pot), 10.1 cm (butter-dish),
6.2 cm (cream-cup)
Impressed in the paste: *Ауэрбахъ Корчева* (coffee-pot); *А. К.* (butter-dish and cream-cup)
Transferred from the Hermitage in 1932
Reproduced for the first time
Inv. Nos. Фс 96, Фс 131, Фс 116, Фс 118

153, 154 Part of the Alexandria services. 1830s

Imperial Porcelain Factory, St. Petersburg
Acquired in 1963
Decanter and wine-glass
Crystal glass, painting in enamel and gold.
Height 21.4 cm, 10.5 cm
Inv. Nos. Ст 3137, Ст 3143
Coffee-pot, creamer, cup and saucer
Porcelain, overglaze painting, gilding. Height 20.5 cm (coffee-pot), 10.5 cm (creamer), 7.5 cm (cup); diam. 13.7 cm (saucer)
Marks in underglaze blue: H_I under the Imperial crown (coffee-pot and cup); the same marks in underglaze green and the date *1854* (creamer)
Inv. Nos. Ф 9463, Ф 9466, Ф 9468

155 Decanter and wine-glass. First half of the 19th century

Two-layered glass. Height 31.6 cm, 12.1 cm
Received from the State Museum Reserve in 1928
Inv. Nos. Ст 801, Ст 817

156 Tulip-shaped glass and saucer-shaped glass. First half of the 19th century

Two-layered glass. Height 14.8 cm, 12 cm
Transferred from the Hermitage in 1939 (tulip-shaped glass). Inv. Nos. Ст 1407, Ст 1396

157 Tea set. 1830—1840s

Imperial Porcelain Factory, St. Petersburg
Porcelain, overglaze and underglaze painting, moulded decoration. Height 17.5 cm (tea-pot), 10 cm (cup with lid), 14.7 cm (sugar-bowl); diam. 60 cm (biscuit-dish)
Transferred from the Hermitage in 1932
Reproduced for the first time
Inv. Nos. Ф 3008, Ф 3013, Ф 3010, Ф 3011

158 Porcelain-framed mirror. 1830—1840s

Imperial Porcelain Factory, St. Petersburg
Porcelain, overglaze painting, moulded decoration.
56 × 40 cm
Transferred from the Hermitage in 1938
Reproduced for the first time
Inv. No. Ф 4446

159 "Esmeralda". Mid-19th century

The Miklashevsky Factory, Chernigov province
Porcelain, overglaze decorative painting. Height 23.6 cm
Mark in overglaze red: *AM*
Transferred from the Hermitage in 1932
Reproduced for the first time
Inv. No. Ф 5831

160 Vase. Mid-19th century

The Miklashevsky Factory, Chernigov province
Porcelain, overglaze painting, gilding and moulded décor.
Height 38 cm
Mark in overglaze: *A. M.*
Transferred from the Hermitage in 1932
Reproduced for the first time
Inv. No. Ф 5844

161 Vase. Mid-19th century

Two-layered glass, painting in enamels, gold and silver.
Height 20.6 cm
Transferred from the Hermitage in 1938
Reproduced for the first time
Inv. No. Ст 950

162 Wine set. 1894—96

The Ovchinnikov Factory, Moscow
Filigreed silver and enamel with gilding.
13.5 × 14 cm (bowl); diam. 34 cm (tray); height 4.8 cm (drinking-cups)

Hallmarks: the emblem of Moscow; *П. Овчинниковъ* for the owner of the factory; above the date, *1896*, the initials *ЛО* for an unidentified tester, active 1890—96; the state emblem of Russia; above the date, *1894*, the unidentified initials *AA*
Acquired in 1965
Reproduced for the first time
Inv. No. Cep 2039—2047

163 Vase. Mid-19th century

Imperial Porcelain Factory, St. Petersburg
Porcelain, overglaze painting, gilding. Height 37.2 cm
Mark in underglaze: *H 1*
Acquired in 1932
Reproduced for the first time
Inv. No. Ф 4072

164 Part of a coffee set. 1908—13

Imperial Porcelain Factory, St. Petersburg
Porcelain, overglaze painting, gilding. 32 × 25.9 cm (tray); height 8.2 cm (cup), 13.8 cm (creamer); diam. 13.4 cm (saucer)
Mark in overglaze green: *HII* and the date *1908* (creamer)
Inscription: *И. X. 1913 г.* (tray)
Transferred from the Catherine Palace (city of Pushkin) in 1932
Inv. Nos. Ф 4970, Ф 4976, Ф 4979, Ф 4980

165 Decorative dish "Sadko". 1899—1900

By M. Vrubel
The Abramtsevo Pottery Works, Moscow province
Majolica, painting, restorative firing. Diam. 88 cm
Acquired in 1963
Reproduced for the first time
Inv. No. Фс 1461

166 Vase. 1912

Imperial Glass Works, St. Petersburg
Multi-layered glass, carving. Height 24.3 cm
Reproduced for the first time
Inv. No. Ст 1943

167 "Lady with a Mask". 1906

By K. Somov
Imperial Porcelain Factory, St. Petersburg
Porcelain, overglaze painting, gilding. Height 22.5 cm
Transferred from the Hermitage in 1938
Inv. No. Ф 5199

168 "The Rape of Europa". 1911

By V. Serov
Porcelain. 24 × 25 × 40.2 cm
Received from the Lomonosov Porcelain Factory, Leningrad, in 1935
Inv. No. Сф 278

169 "Head of a Lioness". 1891

By M. Vrubel
The Abramtsevo Pottery Works, Moscow province
Majolica. 43 × 49 × 27 cm
Acquired from a private collection in 1926
Inv. No. СК 933

170 Panel. Late 19th — early 20th centuries. Detail

Dyed canvas, cotton, silk. Satin-stitch embroidery. 178 × 90.5 cm
Reproduced for the first time
Inv. No. Тк ВХ/ОНР

171 Vase. 1902

By A. Lapshin
Imperial Porcelain Factory, St. Petersburg
Porcelain, underglaze painting. Height 18 cm
Mark in underglaze green: the letters *HII* under the Imperial crown and the date *1902*. Maker's signature: *А. Лапшин*
Transferred from the Hermitage in 1938
Reproduced for the first time
Inv. No. Ф 4772

RUSSIAN APPLIED ART:
Eighteenth to Early Twentieth Century
The Russian Museum, Leningrad

Compiled and introduced by E. Ivanova
Notes on the plates by E. Ivanova, S. Rakhimova
and I. Yasinskaya
Aurora Art Publishers, Leningrad, 1976

РУССКОЕ ПРИКЛАДНОЕ ИСКУССТВО
XVIII — начала XX века

Автор вступительной статьи и составитель Е. Иванова
Авторы аннотаций Е. Иванова, С. Рахимова, И. Ясинская
Издательство «Аврора», Ленинград, 1976

Оформление художника Б. Н. Осенчакова
Фотограф В. А. Стукалов
Перевод Ю. И. Немецкого. Редактор М. Н. Кузнецова
Редакторы английского текста Э. Г. Андреева, И. Б. Комарова
Художественный редактор А. Р. Шилов
Технический редактор Э. С. Кежа
Корректор И. Н. Стукалина

Подписано в печать 25/I 1975. Формат 60×90¹/₈. Бумага мелованная.
Печ. л. 25. Уч.-изд. л. 23,10. Изд. № 50. (11-95). Заказ 9364. Издательство «Аврора». 191065, Ленинград, Невский пр., 7/9. Ордена Трудового Красного Знамени ленинградская типография № 3 имени Ивана Федорова Союзполиграфпрома при Государственном комитете Совета Министров СССР по делам издательств, полиграфии и книжной торговли. 196126, Ленинград, Звенигородская, 11. Ленинградская фабрика офсетной печати № 1. 197101, Ленинград, Кронверкская, 7. Ленинградское производственное объединение «Полиграфоформление». 199161, Ленинград, наб. р. Смоленки, 14
Printed in the USSR